T0054862

The European Union: A Very Short Introduction

VERY SHORT INTRODUCTIONS are for anyone wanting a stimulating and accessible way into a new subject. They are written by experts, and have been translated into more than 45 different languages.

The series began in 1995, and now covers a wide variety of topics in every discipline. The VSI library currently contains over 500 volumes—a Very Short Introduction to everything from Psychology and Philosophy of Science to American History and Relativity—and continues to grow in every subject area.

Very Short Introductions available now:

ACCOUNTING Christopher Nobes
ADOLESCENCE Peter K. Smith
ADVERTISING Winston Fletcher
AFRICAN AMERICAN RELIGION
    Eddie S. Glaude Jr
AFRICAN HISTORY John Parker and
    Richard Rathbone
AFRICAN RELIGIONS Jacob K. Olupona
AGEING Nancy A. Pachana
AGNOSTICISM Robin Le Poidevin
AGRICULTURE Paul Brassley and
    Richard Soffe
ALEXANDER THE GREAT
    Hugh Bowden
ALGEBRA Peter M. Higgins
AMERICAN HISTORY Paul S. Boyer
AMERICAN IMMIGRATION
    David A. Gerber
AMERICAN LEGAL HISTORY
    G. Edward White
AMERICAN POLITICAL HISTORY
    Donald Critchlow
AMERICAN POLITICAL PARTIES
    AND ELECTIONS L. Sandy Maisel
AMERICAN POLITICS Richard M. Valelly
THE AMERICAN PRESIDENCY
    Charles O. Jones
THE AMERICAN REVOLUTION
    Robert J. Allison
AMERICAN SLAVERY
    Heather Andrea Williams
THE AMERICAN WEST Stephen Aron
AMERICAN WOMEN'S HISTORY
    Susan Ware

ANAESTHESIA Aidan O'Donnell
ANALYTIC PHILOSOPHY
    Michael Beaney
ANARCHISM Colin Ward
ANCIENT ASSYRIA Karen Radner
ANCIENT EGYPT Ian Shaw
ANCIENT EGYPTIAN ART AND
    ARCHITECTURE Christina Riggs
ANCIENT GREECE Paul Cartledge
THE ANCIENT NEAR EAST
    Amanda H. Podany
ANCIENT PHILOSOPHY Julia Annas
ANCIENT WARFARE
    Harry Sidebottom
ANGELS David Albert Jones
ANGLICANISM Mark Chapman
THE ANGLO-SAXON AGE John Blair
ANIMAL BEHAVIOUR
    Tristram D. Wyatt
THE ANIMAL KINGDOM
    Peter Holland
ANIMAL RIGHTS David DeGrazia
THE ANTARCTIC Klaus Dodds
ANTISEMITISM Steven Beller
ANXIETY Daniel Freeman and
    Jason Freeman
THE APOCRYPHAL GOSPELS
    Paul Foster
ARCHAEOLOGY Paul Bahn
ARCHITECTURE Andrew Ballantyne
ARISTOCRACY William Doyle
ARISTOTLE Jonathan Barnes
ART HISTORY Dana Arnold
ART THEORY Cynthia Freeland

ASIAN AMERICAN HISTORY
    Madeline Y. Hsu
ASTROBIOLOGY David C. Catling
ASTROPHYSICS James Binney
ATHEISM Julian Baggini
THE ATMOSPHERE Paul I. Palmer
AUGUSTINE Henry Chadwick
AUSTRALIA Kenneth Morgan
AUTISM Uta Frith
THE AVANT GARDE David Cottington
THE AZTECS David Carrasco
BABYLONIA Trevor Bryce
BACTERIA Sebastian G. B. Amyes
BANKING John Goddard and
    John O. S. Wilson
BARTHES Jonathan Culler
THE BEATS David Sterritt
BEAUTY Roger Scruton
BEHAVIOURAL ECONOMICS
    Michelle Baddeley
BESTSELLERS John Sutherland
THE BIBLE John Riches
BIBLICAL ARCHAEOLOGY Eric H. Cline
BIG DATA Dawn E. Holmes
BIOGRAPHY Hermione Lee
BLACK HOLES Katherine Blundell
BLOOD Chris Cooper
THE BLUES Elijah Wald
THE BODY Chris Shilling
THE BOOK OF MORMON
    Terryl Givens
BORDERS Alexander C. Diener and
    Joshua Hagen
THE BRAIN Michael O'Shea
BRANDING Robert Jones
THE BRICS Andrew F. Cooper
THE BRITISH CONSTITUTION
    Martin Loughlin
THE BRITISH EMPIRE Ashley Jackson
BRITISH POLITICS Anthony Wright
BUDDHA Michael Carrithers
BUDDHISM Damien Keown
BUDDHIST ETHICS Damien Keown
BYZANTIUM Peter Sarris
CALVINISM Jon Balserak
CANCER Nicholas James
CAPITALISM James Fulcher
CATHOLICISM Gerald O'Collins
CAUSATION Stephen Mumford and
    Rani Lill Anjum

THE CELL Terence Allen and
    Graham Cowling
THE CELTS Barry Cunliffe
CHAOS Leonard Smith
CHEMISTRY Peter Atkins
CHILD PSYCHOLOGY Usha Goswami
CHILDREN'S LITERATURE
    Kimberley Reynolds
CHINESE LITERATURE Sabina Knight
CHOICE THEORY Michael Allingham
CHRISTIAN ART Beth Williamson
CHRISTIAN ETHICS D. Stephen Long
CHRISTIANITY Linda Woodhead
CIRCADIAN RHYTHMS
    Russell Foster and Leon Kreitzman
CITIZENSHIP Richard Bellamy
CIVIL ENGINEERING
    David Muir Wood
CLASSICAL LITERATURE William Allan
CLASSICAL MYTHOLOGY
    Helen Morales
CLASSICS Mary Beard and
    John Henderson
CLAUSEWITZ Michael Howard
CLIMATE Mark Maslin
CLIMATE CHANGE Mark Maslin
CLINICAL PSYCHOLOGY
    Susan Llewelyn and
    Katie Aafjes-van Doorn
COGNITIVE NEUROSCIENCE
    Richard Passingham
THE COLD WAR Robert McMahon
COLONIAL AMERICA Alan Taylor
COLONIAL LATIN AMERICAN
    LITERATURE Rolena Adorno
COMBINATORICS Robin Wilson
COMEDY Matthew Bevis
COMMUNISM Leslie Holmes
COMPLEXITY John H. Holland
THE COMPUTER Darrel Ince
COMPUTER SCIENCE
    Subrata Dasgupta
CONFUCIANISM Daniel K. Gardner
THE CONQUISTADORS
    Matthew Restall and
    Felipe Fernández-Armesto
CONSCIENCE Paul Strohm
CONSCIOUSNESS Susan Blackmore
CONTEMPORARY ART
    Julian Stallabrass

CONTEMPORARY FICTION
Robert Eaglestone
CONTINENTAL PHILOSOPHY
Simon Critchley
COPERNICUS Owen Gingerich
CORAL REEFS Charles Sheppard
CORPORATE SOCIAL
RESPONSIBILITY
Jeremy Moon
CORRUPTION Leslie Holmes
COSMOLOGY Peter Coles
CRIME FICTION Richard Bradford
CRIMINAL JUSTICE Julian V. Roberts
CRITICAL THEORY
Stephen Eric Bronner
THE CRUSADES Christopher Tyerman
CRYPTOGRAPHY Fred Piper and
Sean Murphy
CRYSTALLOGRAPHY A. M. Glazer
THE CULTURAL REVOLUTION
Richard Curt Kraus
DADA AND SURREALISM
David Hopkins
DANTE Peter Hainsworth and
David Robey
DARWIN Jonathan Howard
THE DEAD SEA SCROLLS
Timothy H. Lim
DECOLONIZATION Dane Kennedy
DEMOCRACY Bernard Crick
DEPRESSION Jan Scott and
Mary Jane Tacchi
DERRIDA Simon Glendinning
DESCARTES Tom Sorell
DESERTS Nick Middleton
DESIGN John Heskett
DEVELOPMENTAL BIOLOGY
Lewis Wolpert
THE DEVIL Darren Oldridge
DIASPORA Kevin Kenny
DICTIONARIES Lynda Mugglestone
DINOSAURS David Norman
DIPLOMACY Joseph M. Siracusa
DOCUMENTARY FILM
Patricia Aufderheide
DREAMING J. Allan Hobson
DRUGS Les Iversen
DRUIDS Barry Cunliffe
EARLY MUSIC Thomas Forrest Kelly
THE EARTH Martin Redfern

EARTH SYSTEM SCIENCE Tim Lenton
ECONOMICS Partha Dasgupta
EDUCATION Gary Thomas
EGYPTIAN MYTH Geraldine Pinch
EIGHTEENTH-CENTURY BRITAIN
Paul Langford
THE ELEMENTS Philip Ball
EMOTION Dylan Evans
EMPIRE Stephen Howe
ENGELS Terrell Carver
ENGINEERING David Blockley
ENGLISH LITERATURE Jonathan Bate
THE ENLIGHTENMENT
John Robertson
ENTREPRENEURSHIP
Paul Westhead and Mike Wright
ENVIRONMENTAL ECONOMICS
Stephen Smith
ENVIRONMENTAL LAW
Elizabeth Fisher
ENVIRONMENTAL POLITICS
Andrew Dobson
EPICUREANISM Catherine Wilson
EPIDEMIOLOGY Rodolfo Saracci
ETHICS Simon Blackburn
ETHNOMUSICOLOGY Timothy Rice
THE ETRUSCANS Christopher Smith
EUGENICS Philippa Levine
THE EUROPEAN UNION
Simon Usherwood and John Pinder
EUROPEAN UNION LAW
Anthony Arnull
EVOLUTION Brian and
Deborah Charlesworth
EXISTENTIALISM Thomas Flynn
EXPLORATION Stewart A. Weaver
THE EYE Michael Land
FAMILY LAW Jonathan Herring
FASCISM Kevin Passmore
FASHION Rebecca Arnold
FEMINISM Margaret Walters
FILM Michael Wood
FILM MUSIC Kathryn Kalinak
THE FIRST WORLD WAR
Michael Howard
FOLK MUSIC Mark Slobin
FOOD John Krebs
FORENSIC PSYCHOLOGY
David Canter
FORENSIC SCIENCE Jim Fraser

FORESTS Jaboury Ghazoul
FOSSILS Keith Thomson
FOUCAULT Gary Gutting
THE FOUNDING FATHERS
    R. B. Bernstein
FRACTALS Kenneth Falconer
FREE SPEECH Nigel Warburton
FREE WILL Thomas Pink
FREEMASONRY Andreas Önnerfors
FRENCH LITERATURE John D. Lyons
THE FRENCH REVOLUTION
    William Doyle
FREUD Anthony Storr
FUNDAMENTALISM Malise Ruthven
FUNGI Nicholas P. Money
THE FUTURE Jennifer M. Gidley
GALAXIES John Gribbin
GALILEO Stillman Drake
GAME THEORY Ken Binmore
GANDHI Bhikhu Parekh
GENES Jonathan Slack
GENIUS Andrew Robinson
GEOGRAPHY John Matthews and
    David Herbert
GEOPOLITICS Klaus Dodds
GERMAN LITERATURE Nicholas Boyle
GERMAN PHILOSOPHY
    Andrew Bowie
GLOBAL CATASTROPHES Bill McGuire
GLOBAL ECONOMIC HISTORY
    Robert C. Allen
GLOBALIZATION Manfred Steger
GOD John Bowker
GOETHE Ritchie Robertson
THE GOTHIC Nick Groom
GOVERNANCE Mark Bevir
GRAVITY Timothy Clifton
THE GREAT DEPRESSION AND
    THE NEW DEAL Eric Rauchway
HABERMAS James Gordon Finlayson
THE HABSBURG EMPIRE Martyn Rady
HAPPINESS Daniel M. Haybron
THE HARLEM RENAISSANCE
    Cheryl A. Wall
THE HEBREW BIBLE AS LITERATURE
    Tod Linafelt
HEGEL Peter Singer
HEIDEGGER Michael Inwood
HEREDITY John Waller
HERMENEUTICS Jens Zimmermann

HERODOTUS Jennifer T. Roberts
HIEROGLYPHS Penelope Wilson
HINDUISM Kim Knott
HISTORY John H. Arnold
THE HISTORY OF ASTRONOMY
    Michael Hoskin
THE HISTORY OF CHEMISTRY
    William H. Brock
THE HISTORY OF CINEMA
    Geoffrey Nowell-Smith
THE HISTORY OF LIFE Michael Benton
THE HISTORY OF MATHEMATICS
    Jacqueline Stedall
THE HISTORY OF MEDICINE
    William Bynum
THE HISTORY OF TIME
    Leofranc Holford-Strevens
HIV AND AIDS Alan Whiteside
HOBBES Richard Tuck
HOLLYWOOD Peter Decherney
HOME Michael Allen Fox
HORMONES Martin Luck
HUMAN ANATOMY
    Leslie Klenerman
HUMAN EVOLUTION Bernard Wood
HUMAN RIGHTS Andrew Clapham
HUMANISM Stephen Law
HUME A. J. Ayer
HUMOUR Noël Carroll
THE ICE AGE Jamie Woodward
IDEOLOGY Michael Freeden
THE IMMUNE SYSTEM
    Paul Klenerman
INDIAN CINEMA Ashish Rajadhyaksha
INDIAN PHILOSOPHY Sue Hamilton
THE INDUSTRIAL REVOLUTION
    Robert C. Allen
INFECTIOUS DISEASE Marta L. Wayne
    and Benjamin M. Bolker
INFINITY Ian Stewart
INFORMATION Luciano Floridi
INNOVATION Mark Dodgson
    and David Gann
INTELLIGENCE Ian J. Deary
INTELLECTUAL PROPERTY
    Siva Vaidhyanathan
INTERNATIONAL LAW
    Vaughan Lowe
INTERNATIONAL MIGRATION
    Khalid Koser

INTERNATIONAL RELATIONS
    Paul Wilkinson
INTERNATIONAL SECURITY
    Christopher S. Browning
IRAN Ali M. Ansari
ISLAM Malise Ruthven
ISLAMIC HISTORY Adam Silverstein
ISOTOPES Rob Ellam
ITALIAN LITERATURE
    Peter Hainsworth and David Robey
JESUS Richard Bauckham
JEWISH HISTORY David N. Myers
JOURNALISM Ian Hargreaves
JUDAISM Norman Solomon
JUNG Anthony Stevens
KABBALAH Joseph Dan
KAFKA Ritchie Robertson
KANT Roger Scruton
KEYNES Robert Skidelsky
KIERKEGAARD Patrick Gardiner
KNOWLEDGE Jennifer Nagel
THE KORAN Michael Cook
LANDSCAPE ARCHITECTURE
    Ian H. Thompson
LANDSCAPES AND
    GEOMORPHOLOGY
    Andrew Goudie and Heather Viles
LANGUAGES Stephen R. Anderson
LATE ANTIQUITY Gillian Clark
LAW Raymond Wacks
THE LAWS OF THERMODYNAMICS
    Peter Atkins
LEADERSHIP Keith Grint
LEARNING Mark Haselgrove
LEIBNIZ Maria Rosa Antognazza
LIBERALISM Michael Freeden
LIGHT Ian Walmsley
LINCOLN Allen C. Guelzo
LINGUISTICS Peter Matthews
LITERARY THEORY Jonathan Culler
LOCKE John Dunn
LOGIC Graham Priest
LOVE Ronald de Sousa
MACHIAVELLI Quentin Skinner
MADNESS Andrew Scull
MAGIC Owen Davies
MAGNA CARTA Nicholas Vincent
MAGNETISM Stephen Blundell
MALTHUS Donald Winch
MAMMALS T. S. Kemp

MANAGEMENT John Hendry
MAO Delia Davin
MARINE BIOLOGY Philip V. Mladenov
THE MARQUIS DE SADE John Phillips
MARTIN LUTHER Scott H. Hendrix
MARTYRDOM Jolyon Mitchell
MARX Peter Singer
MATERIALS Christopher Hall
MATHEMATICS Timothy Gowers
THE MEANING OF LIFE
    Terry Eagleton
MEASUREMENT David Hand
MEDICAL ETHICS Tony Hope
MEDICAL LAW Charles Foster
MEDIEVAL BRITAIN John Gillingham
    and Ralph A. Griffiths
MEDIEVAL LITERATURE
    Elaine Treharne
MEDIEVAL PHILOSOPHY
    John Marenbon
MEMORY Jonathan K. Foster
METAPHYSICS Stephen Mumford
THE MEXICAN REVOLUTION
    Alan Knight
MICHAEL FARADAY
    Frank A. J. L. James
MICROBIOLOGY Nicholas P. Money
MICROECONOMICS Avinash Dixit
MICROSCOPY Terence Allen
THE MIDDLE AGES Miri Rubin
MILITARY JUSTICE Eugene R. Fidell
MILITARY STRATEGY
    Antulio J. Echevarria II
MINERALS David Vaughan
MIRACLES Yujin Nagasawa
MODERN ART David Cottington
MODERN CHINA Rana Mitter
MODERN DRAMA
    Kirsten E. Shepherd-Barr
MODERN FRANCE
    Vanessa R. Schwartz
MODERN INDIA Craig Jeffrey
MODERN IRELAND Senia Pašeta
MODERN ITALY Anna Cento Bull
MODERN JAPAN
    Christopher Goto-Jones
MODERN LATIN AMERICAN
    LITERATURE
    Roberto González Echevarría
MODERN WAR Richard English

MODERNISM Christopher Butler
MOLECULAR BIOLOGY Aysha Divan
    and Janice A. Royds
MOLECULES Philip Ball
MONASTICISM Stephen J. Davis
THE MONGOLS Morris Rossabi
MOONS David A. Rothery
MORMONISM Richard Lyman Bushman
MOUNTAINS Martin F. Price
MUHAMMAD Jonathan A. C. Brown
MULTICULTURALISM Ali Rattansi
MULTILINGUALISM John C. Maher
MUSIC Nicholas Cook
MYTH Robert A. Segal
THE NAPOLEONIC WARS
    Mike Rapport
NATIONALISM Steven Grosby
NAVIGATION Jim Bennett
NELSON MANDELA Elleke Boehmer
NEOLIBERALISM Manfred Steger
    and Ravi Roy
NETWORKS Guido Caldarelli
    and Michele Catanzaro
THE NEW TESTAMENT
    Luke Timothy Johnson
THE NEW TESTAMENT AS
    LITERATURE Kyle Keefer
NEWTON Robert Iliffe
NIETZSCHE Michael Tanner
NINETEENTH-CENTURY BRITAIN
    Christopher Harvie and
    H. C. G. Matthew
THE NORMAN CONQUEST
    George Garnett
NORTH AMERICAN INDIANS
    Theda Perdue and Michael D. Green
NORTHERN IRELAND
    Marc Mulholland
NOTHING Frank Close
NUCLEAR PHYSICS Frank Close
NUCLEAR POWER Maxwell Irvine
NUCLEAR WEAPONS
    Joseph M. Siracusa
NUMBERS Peter M. Higgins
NUTRITION David A. Bender
OBJECTIVITY Stephen Gaukroger
OCEANS Dorrik Stow
THE OLD TESTAMENT
    Michael D. Coogan
THE ORCHESTRA D. Kern Holoman

ORGANIC CHEMISTRY
    Graham Patrick
ORGANIZATIONS Mary Jo Hatch
PAGANISM Owen Davies
PAIN Rob Boddice
THE PALESTINIAN-ISRAELI
    CONFLICT Martin Bunton
PANDEMICS Christian W. McMillen
PARTICLE PHYSICS Frank Close
PAUL E. P. Sanders
PEACE Oliver P. Richmond
PENTECOSTALISM William K. Kay
PERCEPTION Brian Rogers
THE PERIODIC TABLE Eric R. Scerri
PHILOSOPHY Edward Craig
PHILOSOPHY IN THE ISLAMIC
    WORLD Peter Adamson
PHILOSOPHY OF LAW
    Raymond Wacks
PHILOSOPHY OF SCIENCE
    Samir Okasha
PHOTOGRAPHY Steve Edwards
PHYSICAL CHEMISTRY Peter Atkins
PILGRIMAGE Ian Reader
PLAGUE Paul Slack
PLANETS David A. Rothery
PLANTS Timothy Walker
PLATE TECTONICS Peter Molnar
PLATO Julia Annas
POLITICAL PHILOSOPHY
    David Miller
POLITICS Kenneth Minogue
POPULISM Cas Mudde and
    Cristóbal Rovira Kaltwasser
POSTCOLONIALISM Robert Young
POSTMODERNISM Christopher Butler
POSTSTRUCTURALISM
    Catherine Belsey
PREHISTORY Chris Gosden
PRESOCRATIC PHILOSOPHY
    Catherine Osborne
PRIVACY Raymond Wacks
PROBABILITY John Haigh
PROGRESSIVISM Walter Nugent
PROJECTS Andrew Davies
PROTESTANTISM Mark A. Noll
PSYCHIATRY Tom Burns
PSYCHOANALYSIS Daniel Pick
PSYCHOLOGY Gillian Butler and
    Freda McManus

PSYCHOTHERAPY Tom Burns and
    Eva Burns-Lundgren
PUBLIC ADMINISTRATION
    Stella Z. Theodoulou and Ravi K. Roy
PUBLIC HEALTH Virginia Berridge
PURITANISM Francis J. Bremer
THE QUAKERS Pink Dandelion
QUANTUM THEORY
    John Polkinghorne
RACISM Ali Rattansi
RADIOACTIVITY Claudio Tuniz
RASTAFARI Ennis B. Edmonds
THE REAGAN REVOLUTION Gil Troy
REALITY Jan Westerhoff
THE REFORMATION Peter Marshall
RELATIVITY Russell Stannard
RELIGION IN AMERICA Timothy Beal
THE RENAISSANCE Jerry Brotton
RENAISSANCE ART
    Geraldine A. Johnson
REVOLUTIONS Jack A. Goldstone
RHETORIC Richard Toye
RISK Baruch Fischhoff and John Kadvany
RITUAL Barry Stephenson
RIVERS Nick Middleton
ROBOTICS Alan Winfield
ROCKS Jan Zalasiewicz
ROMAN BRITAIN Peter Salway
THE ROMAN EMPIRE
    Christopher Kelly
THE ROMAN REPUBLIC
    David M. Gwynn
ROMANTICISM Michael Ferber
ROUSSEAU Robert Wokler
RUSSELL A. C. Grayling
RUSSIAN HISTORY Geoffrey Hosking
RUSSIAN LITERATURE Catriona Kelly
THE RUSSIAN REVOLUTION
    S. A. Smith
SAVANNAS Peter A. Furley
SCHIZOPHRENIA Chris Frith and
    Eve Johnstone
SCHOPENHAUER Christopher Janaway
SCIENCE AND RELIGION
    Thomas Dixon
SCIENCE FICTION David Seed
THE SCIENTIFIC REVOLUTION
    Lawrence M. Principe
SCOTLAND Rab Houston
SEXUALITY Véronique Mottier

SHAKESPEARE'S COMEDIES
    Bart van Es
SHAKESPEARE'S SONNETS AND
    POEMS Jonathan F. S. Post
SHAKESPEARE'S TRAGEDIES
    Stanley Wells
SIKHISM Eleanor Nesbitt
THE SILK ROAD James A. Millward
SLANG Jonathon Green
SLEEP Steven W. Lockley and
    Russell G. Foster
SOCIAL AND CULTURAL
    ANTHROPOLOGY
    John Monaghan and Peter Just
SOCIAL PSYCHOLOGY Richard J. Crisp
SOCIAL WORK Sally Holland and
    Jonathan Scourfield
SOCIALISM Michael Newman
SOCIOLINGUISTICS John Edwards
SOCIOLOGY Steve Bruce
SOCRATES C. C. W. Taylor
SOUND Mike Goldsmith
THE SOVIET UNION Stephen Lovell
THE SPANISH CIVIL WAR
    Helen Graham
SPANISH LITERATURE Jo Labanyi
SPINOZA Roger Scruton
SPIRITUALITY Philip Sheldrake
SPORT Mike Cronin
STARS Andrew King
STATISTICS David J. Hand
STEM CELLS Jonathan Slack
STRUCTURAL ENGINEERING
    David Blockley
STUART BRITAIN John Morrill
SUPERCONDUCTIVITY
    Stephen Blundell
SYMMETRY Ian Stewart
TAXATION Stephen Smith
TEETH Peter S. Ungar
TELESCOPES Geoff Cottrell
TERRORISM Charles Townshend
THEATRE Marvin Carlson
THEOLOGY David F. Ford
THINKING AND REASONING
    Jonathan St B. T. Evans
THOMAS AQUINAS Fergus Kerr
THOUGHT Tim Bayne
TIBETAN BUDDHISM
    Matthew T. Kapstein

TOCQUEVILLE Harvey C. Mansfield
TRAGEDY Adrian Poole
TRANSLATION Matthew Reynolds
THE TROJAN WAR Eric H. Cline
TRUST Katherine Hawley
THE TUDORS John Guy
TWENTIETH-CENTURY BRITAIN
    Kenneth O. Morgan
THE UNITED NATIONS
    Jussi M. Hanhimäki
UNIVERSITIES AND COLLEGES
    David Palfreyman and Paul Temple
THE U.S. CONGRESS Donald A. Ritchie
THE U.S. SUPREME COURT
    Linda Greenhouse
UTILITARIANISM
    Katarzyna de Lazari-Radek and
    Peter Singer
UTOPIANISM Lyman Tower Sargent
THE VIKINGS Julian Richards

VIRUSES Dorothy H. Crawford
VOLTAIRE Nicholas Cronk
WAR AND TECHNOLOGY
    Alex Roland
WATER John Finney
WEATHER Storm Dunlop
THE WELFARE STATE David Garland
WILLIAM SHAKESPEARE
    Stanley Wells
WITCHCRAFT Malcolm Gaskill
WITTGENSTEIN A. C. Grayling
WORK Stephen Fineman
WORLD MUSIC Philip Bohlman
THE WORLD TRADE
    ORGANIZATION
    Amrita Narlikar
WORLD WAR II Gerhard L. Weinberg
WRITING AND SCRIPT
    Andrew Robinson
ZIONISM Michael Stanislawski

Available soon:

VETERINARY SCIENCE
    James Yeates
THE ENGLISH LANGUAGE
    Simon Horobin
FAIRY TALES Marina Warner

ORGANISED CRIME
    Georgios A. Antonopoulos and
    Georgios Papanicolaou
THE PHILOSOPHY OF RELIGION
    Tim Bayne

For more information visit our website

www.oup.com/vsi/

Simon Usherwood and John Pinder

THE EUROPEAN UNION

A Very Short Introduction

FOURTH EDITION

OXFORD

UNIVERSITY PRESS

Great Clarendon Street, Oxford, OX2 6DP,
United Kingdom

Oxford University Press is a department of the University of Oxford.
It furthers the University's objective of excellence in research, scholarship,
and education by publishing worldwide. Oxford is a registered trade mark of
Oxford University Press in the UK and in certain other countries

First edition published 2001.
Second edition published 2007.
Third edition published 2013.
This edition published 2018.

Published in the United States of America by Oxford University Press
198 Madison Avenue, New York, NY 10016, United States of America

British Library Cataloguing in Publication Data
Data available

Library of Congress Control Number: 2017950312

ISBN 978-0-19-880885-5

Printed and bound by CPI Group (UK) Ltd, Croydon, CR0 4YY

Links to third party websites are provided by Oxford in good faith and
for information only. Oxford disclaims any responsibility for the materials
contained in any third party website referenced in this work.

Contents

Foreword xv

Abbreviations xvii

List of boxes xxi

List of charts xxiii

List of illustrations xxv

List of maps xxvii

1 What the EU is for 1

2 How the EU was made 9

3 How the EU is governed 34

4 Single market, single currency 56

5 Agriculture, regions, budget: conflicts over who gets what 69

6 Social policy, environmental policy 83

7 'An area of freedom, security and justice' 89

8 A great civilian power…and more—or less? 96

9   The EU and the rest of Europe 109

10   The EU in the world 121

11   Much accomplished...but what next? 138

References 149

Further reading 151

Chronology: 1946–2017 153

Glossary 161

Index 169

Foreword

This fourth edition is a more sombre affair than its predecessors, for several reasons. Most obviously, the political and social developments since the previous edition have given much cause to question the rather optimistic take on affairs, most clearly seen in the UK's 2016 referendum decision to leave the EU. Coupled to this we see a continued rise in populism across the continent; the challenges posed by immigration flows; an unsteady Russia (and, more recently, US); and a Eurozone soon to mark a decade of sclerosis. As ever, this requires this slim volume to cover even more than before, something that has required some trimming back of previous content.

More personally, I have to mourn the passing of John Pinder in 2015, just one month before the British general election that was to lead to the UK's decision. John's career and experience is almost too vast to contemplate, from the Second World War to moving among the federalist community for many decades, as both scholar and advocate. He is sorely missed not only by myself, but by his many colleagues and friends, and I consider it a privilege to co-author possibly the last book to bear his name. And this remains very much John's book, reflecting still his view of a pragmatic movement in Europe towards a more federal model of governance. Bathetic though the events since John's death might appear, I hope that I can offer a balanced and fair view.

As always, my concern has been to present the ideas in a way that will help to provide a context for reasonable people, whatever their views, to evaluate the performance of the EU and judge in which direction it should go. And I have endeavoured to be scrupulous about the facts.

With all of this in mind, I owe thanks to even more people than before, including Angus Armstrong, Catherine Barnard, Iain Begg, Laura Chappell, Brendan Connelly, Helen Drake, Andrew Duff, Theofanis Exadaktylos, Roberta Guerrina, Nigel Haigh, Christopher Johnson, Anand Menon, Jörg Monar, Simon Nuttall, Richard Whitman, and Jon Worth. OUP have continued to combine their efficiency with a thoughtful support of the changing situation. If what follows does not please the reader, it is no fault of theirs.

June 2017
Simon Usherwood

Abbreviations

ACP	African, Caribbean, Pacific countries
AFSJ	Area of Freedom, Security and Justice
Benelux	Belgium, Netherlands, and Luxembourg
CAP	common agricultural policy
CFSP	Common Foreign and Security Policy
CIS	Commonwealth of Independent States
CJHA	Cooperation in Justice and Home Affairs
Coreper	Committee of Permanent Representatives
CSDP	Common Security and Defence Policy
EAGGF	European Agricultural Guidance and Guarantee Fund
EC	European Community
ECB	European Central Bank
ECJ	European Court of Justice (formal title, Court of Justice)
Ecofin	Council of Economic and Finance Ministers
Ecosoc	Economic and Social Committee
ECSC	European Coal and Steel Community
ecu	European Currency Unit (forerunner of euro)
EDC	European Defence Community
EDF	European Development Fund
EEA	European Economic Area
EEC	European Economic Community
EFSF	European Financial Stabilty Fund
Efta	European Free Trade Association

EMS	European Monetary System
Emu	Economic and Monetary Union
ENP	European Neighbourhood Policy
EPC	European Political Cooperation
ERDF	European Regional Development Fund
ERM	Exchange Rate Mechanism
ESCB	European System of Central Banks
ESDP	European Security and Defence Policy
ESF	European Social Fund
ESM	European Stability Mechanism
EU	European Union
Euratom	European Atomic Energy Community
Gatt	General Agreement on Tariffs and Trade (forerunner of WTO)
GDP	Gross Domestic Product
GNI	Gross National Income
GNP	Gross National Product
GSP	Generalized System of Preferences
IGC	Intergovernmental Conference
MEP	member of the European Parliament
Nato	North Atlantic Treaty Organization
NTBs	non-tariff barriers
OECD	Organisation for Economic Co-operation and Development
OMC	open method of coordination
OSCE	Organization for Security and Co-operation in Europe
PHARE	Poland and Hungary: aid for economic reconstruction (extended to other Central and Eastern European countries)
QMV	qualified majority voting (in the Council of Ministers)
SEA	Single European Act
SFP	Single Farm Payment
TACIS	Technical Assistance to the CIS
TEC	Treaty establishing the European Community
TEU	Treaty on European Union

TFEU	Treaty on the Functioning of the European Union
TSCG	Treaty on Stability, Coordination and Governance in the Economic and Monetary Union
UN	United Nations
VAT	value-added tax
WEU	Western European Union
WTO	World Trade Organization

TRIPS   Agreement on Trade-Related Aspects of
        Intellectual Property

        Customs and Excise

VAT   Value Added Tax
PPP   Public Private Partnership
WTO   World Trade Organization

List of boxes

1 The treaties **13**

2 Structural funds and objectives **75**

3 States' net budgetary payments or receipts **81**

4 Employment policy **86**

5 Cotonou Convention, 2000–20 **126**

6 EU international agreements beyond Cotonou and ENP **130**

List of charts

1   Number of MEPs from each
    state, 2017 **41**

2   Party groups in the Parliament
    in 2017 **42**

3   Share of budget spent
    on agriculture, 1970–2020 **72**

4   Breakdown of budget
    expenditure, 2015
    (€ billion) **77**

5   Sources of revenue, 2015 **79**

6   Shares of world merchandise
    trade of the EU, the US, China,
    Japan, and others, 2015 **99**

7   Direction of EU trade by
    region, 2015 **124**

8   Shares of official development
    aid from the EU, the US,
    Japan, and others (2014) **131**

9   Development aid from the EU
    and member states by
    destination, 2014 **132**

List of illustrations

1 Churchill at The Hague **6**
Photo by Kurt Hutton / Picture Post /
Hulton Archive / Getty Images

2 Monnet and Schuman **11**
Photo © AGIP / Bridgeman Images

3 British entry **18**
Photo by Douglas Miller / Keystone /
Hulton Archive / Getty Images

4 Delors **19**
© European Communities, 1994 /
Source: EC—Audiovisual Service /
Photo: Christian Lambiotte

5 Remembering Altiero Spinelli
at Ventotene, August 2016 **22**
Photo by Tiberio Barchielli / Italian
Prime Ministery / Anadolu Agency /
Getty Images

6 The EU's institutions **35**

7 European Council 1979 **36**
Photo by Keystone / Hulton Archive /
Getty Images

8 Elected representatives at
work **44**
European Parliament

9 The Juncker Commission **48**
© European Union 2014—European
Parliament. (Attribution—
NonCommercial—NoDerivs
Creative Commons license)

10 Institutions of economic and
monetary policy **63**

11 Kohl and Mitterrand hold
hands at Verdun cemetery **103**
© Bettmann / Getty Images

12 How the EU is represented for
Common Foreign and Security
Policy **105**

13 The informal meeting of the
Union's leaders in Bratislava
in September 2016, to discuss
the future of the EU; the UK
was not invited **136**
REUTERS / Alamy Stock Photo

14 Europeans in the global
community: national and EU
heads at the G8, May
2012 **144**
© European Union, 2012 / Source:
EC—Audiovisual Service / Photo:
Cornelia Smet

List of maps

1   The changing membership of
     the EU since 1957 **24**

2   Candidates for future
     accession **114**

3   The architecture of Europe,
     2017 **118**

4   The EU's neighbourhood **128**

Chapter 1
What the EU is for

In the simplest of terms, the European Union (EU) is an international organization, founded on treaties between European states. But such a description does not do justice to a body that has grown and developed since the 1950s to cover many areas of public policy and to reach deep into the political, economic, and social lives of its peoples. That change has led some to see it as a proto-state or a new form of political organization altogether, mixing direct representation of citizens with close coordination of national governments. The EU has been driven by and reflected the wider context in which it operates.

One of the paradoxes of the EU is that it appears to be a political upstart, a novel form of governance even as it now enters its seventh decade of existence. As this introductory chapter will discuss, the specific circumstances of its birth have given way to a very different world to which it has sometimes struggled to adapt. If we are to understand why the EU is where it is now then we have to begin with that birth, for its effects have been profound and lasting.

The EU of today is the result of a process that began in the wake of the Second World War with the creation of the European Coal and Steel Community (ECSC). The coal and steel industries then still provided the industrial muscle for military power, with

Robert Schuman, the French Foreign Minister, affirming, on
9 May 1950 in his declaration which launched the project, that
'any war between France and Germany' would become 'not merely
unthinkable, but materially impossible'.

A durable peace

It may not be easy, at today's distance, to appreciate how much this
meant, only five years after the end of the war of 1939–45 that had
brought such terrible suffering to almost all European countries.
For France and Germany, which had been at war with each other
three times in the preceding eight decades, finding a way to live
together in a durable peace was a fundamental political priority
that the new European Community (EC) was designed to serve.

For France the prospect of a completely independent Germany,
with its formidable industrial potential, was alarming. The
attempt to keep Germany down, as the French had tried to do
after the 1914–18 war, had failed disastrously. The idea of binding
Germany within strong institutions, which would equally bind
France and other European countries and thus be acceptable to
Germans over the longer term, seemed more promising. That
promise has been amply fulfilled. The French could regard the
EU as the outcome of their original initiative, and they sought,
with considerable success, to play the part of leader among
European nations, at least during the Cold War era.

But participation in these European institutions on an equal basis
has also given Germany a framework within which to develop
peaceful and constructive relations with the growing number
of other member states, as well as to complete their unification
smoothly in 1990. Following the twelve years of Nazi rule that
ended with devastation in 1945, the EEC offered Germans a way
to become a respected people again. The idea of a community
of equals with strong institutions was attractive. Schuman also
declared that the new EEC would be 'the first concrete foundation

of a European federation which is indispensable to the preservation of peace'. While French commitment to developing the Community in a federal direction has been variable, the German political class has consistently supported it, having thoroughly absorbed the concept of federal democracy. Indeed, in 1992, an amendment to the Basic Law of the reunited Germany provided for its participation in the EU, committed to federal principles.

The other four founder states, Belgium, Italy, Luxembourg, and the Netherlands, also saw the new EEC as a means to ensure peace by binding Germany within strong European institutions. For the most part they too, like the Germans, saw and have largely continued to see the Community as a stage in the development of a federal polity.

Although the Second World War is receding into a more distant past, the motive of peace and security within a democratic polity, fundamental to the foundation of the EEC, remains a powerful influence on governments and politicians in many of the member states. The system that has provided a framework for over half a century of peace is regarded as a means of future stability, something reflected in the thinking of the Nobel committee in their awarding the EU the Nobel Peace Prize in 2012. One means of consolidating peace was the decision to consolidate the EU by introducing a single currency, seen as a way to reinforce the safe anchorage of a potentially more powerful Germany after its unification. Another means was the accession of Central and Eastern European states seeking a safe haven after the Second World War followed by half a century of Soviet domination. This has led to continuing pressure to strengthen the EU's institutions in order to maintain stability as eastern enlargement increases the number of member states well beyond the original six.

The British, having avoided the experience of defeat and occupation, did not share that fundamental motivation for the sharing of sovereignty with other European peoples, feeling a reliance on the United States (US) and Nato (North Atlantic Treaty Organization) to be sufficient. This has resulted in a much more utilitarian approach by successive generations of British politicians: integration was a means of improving trade and securing some common policy objectives rather than a bigger project of modernization or community building. Ironically, despite the ever greater shaping of the EU in line with British priorities—market liberalization, enlargement, Nato-led security—this did not engender any basic change in the British attitude. The 2016 referendum decision for the UK to leave the EU highlights the tensions in this situation very clearly: membership has had both costs and benefits, but it is only at the point of departure that both British politicians and its public discover the full dimensions of their European integration and the entanglements it has created.

Economic strength and prosperity

While a durable peace was a profound political motive for establishing the new EEC, it would not have succeeded without adequate performance in the economic field in which it was given its powers; and the EEC did in fact serve an economic as well as political logic. The frontiers between France, Germany, Belgium, and Luxembourg, standing between steel plants and the mines whose coal they required, impeded rational production; and the removal of those barriers, accompanied by common governance of the resulting common market, was successful in economic terms. This, together with the evidence that peaceful reconciliation among the member states was being achieved, encouraged them to see the ECSC as a first step, as Schuman had indicated, in a process of political as well as economic unification. After an unsuccessful attempt at a second step, when the French National Assembly failed to ratify a treaty for the European Defence Community (EDC) in 1954, the six founder states proceeded again on the path of economic integration. The concept of a common market was extended to the whole of the members' mutual trade in goods when the European Economic Community (EEC) was founded in 1958, opening up the way to an integrated economy that responded to the logic of economic interdependence among the member states.

The EEC was also, thanks to French insistence on surrounding the common market with a common external tariff, able to enter trade negotiations on level terms with the US—thus demonstrating the potential for the EEC to become a major actor on the international stage, when armed with a common means with which to conduct external policy. It was a first step towards satisfying another motive for creating the EEC: to restore European influence in the wider world—an influence that had been dissipated by the two great fratricidal wars, but which could now be reinforced by the EU's potential for contributing to much needed global safety and prosperity.

One exception to those in Britain failing to understand the strength of the case for such radical reform was Winston Churchill (Figure 1) who, less than a year and a half after the end of the war, said in a speech in Zurich: 'We must now build a kind of United States of Europe...the first step must be a partnership between France and Germany...France and Germany must take the lead together.' But few among the British understood so well the case for a new community—and even Churchill did not feel that Britain, being then head of its own empire and with a recently forged special relationship with the US, should be a member. Many were, however, reluctant to be disadvantaged in Continental markets and excluded from taking important policy decisions in Continent Europe. So after failing to secure a free trade area that would incorporate the EEC as well as other Western European countries, successive British governments sought entry into the EEC—finally succeeding in 1973. But while the British played a leading part in developing the common market into a more complete single market, they continued to lack the political

1. **Churchill at The Hague: founds the European Movement, following his call for 'a kind of United States of Europe'.**

motivation that had driven the founder states, as well as some others, to press towards other forms of deeper integration.

It is important to understand the motivations of the founders and of the British, which, while they continue to evolve, still influence attitudes towards the EU. Such motivations are shared, in various proportions, by other states that have joined the EU over the years; and they underlie much of the drama that has unfolded since 1950 to produce the EU that is the subject of this book.

Theories and explanations

There are two main ways of explaining the phenomenon of the EEC and the EU. Adherents to the first emphasize the role of the member states and their intergovernmental dealings; adherents to the second give greater weight to the European institutions.

Most of the former, belonging to the 'realist' or 'neo-realist' schools of thought, hold that the EEC and the EU have not wrought any fundamental change in the relationships between member states, whose governments continue to pursue their national interests and seek as much to maximize their power within the EU as they do elsewhere. A more recent variant, called *liberal intergovernmentalism*, looks to the forces at play in domestic politics to explain the various governments' behaviour in the EU. For want of a better word, 'intergovernmentalist' is used here for this family of explanations as to how the EEC and EU work.

One should not underestimate the role that member state governments retain in EU affairs, with their status as signatories of EU treaties, their power of decision in the Council of Ministers representing member states, and their monopoly of the *ultima ratio* of armed force. But other approaches, including those known as 'neo-functionalist' and 'federalist', give more weight than the intergovernmentalists to European institutions.

Neo-functionalists saw the EEC developing by a process of 'spillover' from the original ECSC, whose scope was confined to only two industrial sectors. Interest groups and political parties, attracted by the success of the Community in dealing with the problems of these two sectors, would become frustrated by its inability to deal with related problems in other fields and would, with leadership from the European Commission, press successfully for the Community's competence to be extended, until it would eventually provide a form of European governance for a wide range of member state affairs. This offers at least a partial explanation of some steps in the Community's development, including the move from a single market to a single currency.

A federalist perspective, while also stressing the importance of the common institutions, goes beyond neo-functionalism in two main ways. First, it relates the transfer of powers to the EU less to a spillover from existing powers to new ones than to a growing inability of governments to deal effectively with problems that have become transnational thus extending beyond the reach of existing states. Most of these transnational problems concern the economy, the environment, and security—states should still retain control over internal matters with which they can still cope adequately. Second, whereas neo-functionalists have not been clear about which principles might shape European institutions, federalists have based their perspectives on principles of liberal democracy: in particular, a rule of law based on fundamental rights; and representative governments with laws enacted and an executive controlled by elected representatives of individual state citizens. In this latter view, powers exercised jointly need to be dealt with by government institutions, because the intergovernmental method is neither effective nor democratic enough to satisfy the needs of citizens of democratic states. So either the federal elements in the institutions will be strengthened until the EU becomes an effective democratic polity, based on the principles of rule of law and representative government; or it will fail to attract enough support from member state citizens to enable it to flourish—or perhaps even to survive. The EU is not designed to replace member states but rather to transform them into integral parts of a cooperative venture: citizens' identities gain a new layer that interacts with their existing member state identity.

Subsequent chapters will try to show how far the development of the EEC and the EU has reflected these different views. In practice, European-level governance has developed so extensively that whatever one's view of which approach should be taken, there is an overriding priority to ensure that the system is in equal measure effective and democratic if it is to have a meaningful future.

Chapter 2
How the EU was made

'Europe will not be made all at once, or according to a single, general plan. It will be built through concrete achievements, which first create a de facto solidarity.' With these words, the Schuman declaration accurately predicted the way in which the Community has become the Union of today. The institutions and powers have been developed step by step, following the confidence gained through the success of preceding steps, to deal with matters that appeared to be best handled by common action.

Other chapters consider particular institutions and fields of competence in more detail. Here we see how interests and events combined to bring about the development as a whole. Some primary interests and motives were considered in Chapter 1: security, not just through military means but by establishing economic and political relationships; prosperity, with business and trade unions particularly interested; protection of the environment, with pressure from green parties and voluntary organizations; and influence in external relations to promote common interests in the wider world.

With the creation of the EEC to serve such purposes other interests came into play. Those who feared damage from certain aspects sought compensation through redistributive measures: for France, the common agricultural policy (CAP) to counterbalance German industrial advantage; the structural funds for countries with weaker economies that feared they would lose from the single market; budgetary adjustments for the British and others with high net contributions. Some governments, parliaments, parties, and voluntary organizations have pressed for reforms aiming to make the institutions more effective and democratic. Against them have stood those who resist moves beyond intergovernmental decision-making, acting from a variety of motives: ideological commitment to the nation-state; a belief that democracy is feasible only within and not beyond it; mistrust of foreigners; and simple attachment to the status quo. Among them have been such historic figures as President de Gaulle and Prime Minister Thatcher, as well as a wide range of institutions and individuals, the most prevalent being British, Danish, Hungarian, and Polish. Among the European institutions, it is the Council of Ministers that has come closest to this view.

Two of the most influential federalists, committed to the development of a European polity that would deal effectively with the common interests of the member states and their citizens, have been Jean Monnet and Jacques Delors. Both initiated major steps towards a federal aim. Altiero Spinelli represented a different kind of federalism, envisaging more radical moves towards a European constitution. The German, Italian, Belgian, and Dutch parliaments and governments have in varying degrees been institutionally federalist, as have the European Commission and Parliament, and, in so far as the treaties could be interpreted in that way, the Court of Justice. They have generally preferred Monnet's stepwise approach.

The 1950s: the founding treaties

Monnet was responsible for drafting the Schuman declaration, chairing the negotiations for the ECSC Treaty, and was the first President of its High Authority (Figure 2). This choice of words for the body reflected his insistence on a strong executive at the centre of the Community, stemming originally from his experience as Deputy Secretary General of the interwar League of Nations which had convinced him of the weakness of an intergovernmental system. He was, however, persuaded that, for democratic member states, such a community should be provided with a parliamentary assembly and a court—embryonic elements of a federal legislature and judiciary—and that there should be a council of ministers representing the member states.

This structure has remained remarkably stable to this day, though the relationship between the institutions has changed: the Council of Ministers, and in particular, since 1974, the European Council of government heads, has become the most powerful; the European Commission, while still very important, has lost ground to it; the European Parliament has gained in power; and the Court of Justice has established itself as the supreme judicial authority in matters of EU competence. Although they were later to accept

2. **Monnet and Schuman.**

these institutions, British governments of the 1950s felt them to be too federal for British participation.

The six member states, however, were minded to proceed further in that direction. The French government reacted to American insistence on German rearmament, following the impact of communist expansionism in both Europe and Korea, by proposing the EDC with a European army. An EDC Treaty was signed by the six governments and ratified by four; but opposition grew in France and the Assemblée Nationale voted in 1954 to shelve it. The result was that the idea of a competence in the field of defence remained a no-go area until the 1990s.

While the collapse of the EDC was a severe setback, confidence in the EEC as a framework for peaceful relations among the member states had grown; and there was a powerful political impulse to 'relaunch' its development. The Dutch were ready with a proposal for a general common market, for which the support of Belgium and Germany was soon forthcoming. The French, still markedly protectionist, were doubtful. But they held to the project of European unification built around Franco-German partnership and so accepted the common market which the Germans wanted, on condition that other French interests were satisfied: an atomic energy community in which France was equipped to play the leading part; the CAP; the association of colonial territories on favourable terms; and equal pay for women throughout the Community, without which French industry, already required by French law to pay it, would in some sectors have been at a competitive disadvantage. The Italians for their part, who had the weakest economy among the six, secured the European Investment Bank, the Social Fund, and free movement of labour. So all these elements were included in the two Rome Treaties, which established the EEC and European Atomic Energy Community (Euratom): an early example of a package deal, incorporating advantages for each member state, which has characterized many of the steps taken since then (see Box 1).

Box 1 The treaties

Rome wasn't built in a day—and the Treaties of Rome (in force in 1958) were a big building block in a long and complicated process that has constructed the present EU. Other major treaties included the ECSC Treaty (in force 1952), Single European Act (1987), Maastricht Treaty (1993), Amsterdam Treaty (1999), Nice Treaty (2002), and Lisbon Treaty (2009).

A minor complication is that there were two Treaties of Rome, but the EEC Treaty was so much more important than the Euratom Treaty that it is generally known as *the* Treaty of Rome.

A major complication is that the EU was set up by the Maastricht Treaty, with two new 'pillars' for foreign policy and internal security alongside the EC, which already had its own treaties. These were organized alongside the TEC, within the TEU. The Lisbon Treaty finally produced some simplification of this, by collapsing all the pillars into one: the EU now operates on the basis of the TEU and the TFEU.

Note: to avoid undue complexity, this book follows two principles in referring to the EC and EU:

- Community, EEC, or EC is used regarding matters relating entirely to the time before the EU was established, or in the period between Maastricht and Lisbon when the EC's separate characteristics are relevant;
- Union or EU in all other cases.

The two new treaties entered into force on 1 January 1958. While Euratom was sidelined, the EEC became the basis for the future development of the Community. Its institutions were similar to those of the ECSC, though with a somewhat less powerful executive, called the 'Commission' instead of the 'High Authority'; and the EEC was given a wide range of economic competences, including the power to establish a customs union with internal free trade and a common external tariff; policies for particular sectors, notably agriculture; and more general cooperation.

The first President of the Commission, Walter Hallstein, led the Commission to a flying start, with acceleration of the timetable for establishing the customs union; and within this framework the EEC enjoyed notable economic success in the 1960s. But conflict between the emergent federal Community, as conceived by Monnet or Hallstein, and de Gaulle's fundamental commitment to the nation-state made that decade politically hazardous for the Community.

The 1960s: de Gaulle against the federalists

In June 1958, less than six months after the Rome Treaties came into force, de Gaulle became the French President. He did not like the federal elements and aspirations of the EEC. But nor was he prepared to challenge directly treaties recently ratified by France. He sought, rather, to use the EEC as a means to advance French power and leadership. One example was his sidelining of Euratom in order to keep the French atomic sector national. Another was his veto which terminated in 1963 the first negotiations to enlarge the EEC to include Britain, Denmark, Ireland, and Norway. Although the British government's conception of the EEC was closer to that of de Gaulle than of the other more federalist-minded member state governments, and Britain's defence of its agricultural and Commonwealth interests had irked the latter by making the negotiations hard and long, they resented the unilateral and nationalist manner of the French veto so deeply that it provoked the first political crisis within the EEC. This was followed, in 1965, by a greater crisis over the arrangements for the CAP.

The CAP had from the outset been a key French interest and de Gaulle was determined to have it established without undue delay. It was to be based on price supports requiring substantial public expenditure. Both France and the Commission agreed that this should come from the budget of the EEC, not that of member states. But the Commission, with its federalist orientation, and the Dutch parliament, with its deep commitment to democratic principles, insisted that the budget spending must be subject to parliamentary control; and since a European budget could not be controlled by six separate parliaments, it would have to be done by the European Parliament. This suited the other governments well enough, but was anathema to de Gaulle. He precipitated the crisis of 'the empty chair', forbidding his ministers to attend meetings of the Council of Ministers throughout the second half of 1965 and evoking fears among the other states that he might be preparing to destroy the EEC.

With neither side being willing to give way, the episode concluded in January 1966 with the so-called 'Luxembourg compromise'. The French government asserted a right of veto when interests 'very important to one or more member states' are at stake; and the other five affirmed their commitment to the treaty provision for qualified majority voting on certain questions, which was that very month due to come into effect for votes on a wide range of subjects. In practice de Gaulle's view prevailed for the next two decades, so that 'Luxembourg veto' seems a more accurate description than 'Luxembourg compromise'. In the mid-1980s, however, majority voting began to be practised in the context of the single market programme, and has now become the standard procedure applicable to most legislative decisions.

Despite these conflicts between intergovernmental and federal conceptions, the customs union was completed by July 1968, earlier than the treaty had required. Its impact had already been felt not only internally but also in the EEC's external relations. Wielding the common instrument of the external tariff, the EEC was becoming, in the field of trade, a power comparable to the US. President Kennedy had reacted by proposing multilateral negotiations for major tariff cuts. Skilfully led by the Commission, the EEC responded positively; and the outcome was cuts averaging one-third, initiating an era in which the EEC was to become the leading force for international trade liberalization.

Alongside the ups and downs of EEC politics, the Court of Justice made steady progress in establishing the rule of law. Based on its treaty obligation to ensure that 'the law is observed', in judgments in 1963 and 1964 the Court established the principles of the primacy and the direct effect of Community law, so that it would be consistently applied in all the member states. Though without the means of enforcement proper to a state, respect for the law, based on the treaties and on legislation enacted by its institutions, provided the cement that has since bound the EC together.

Widening and some deepening: Britain, Denmark, and Ireland join

With de Gaulle's resignation in 1969, French policy became more pragmatic. Britain, Denmark, Ireland, and Norway still sought entry; and the new President, Georges Pompidou, consented, on condition that CAP financing would be agreed as well as elements of 'deepening' such as monetary union and coordination of foreign policy. In addition to serving the French agricultural interest, these were intended to integrate Germany yet more firmly into the EEC, as well as to guard against the danger that widening the EEC would also weaken it. This fitted well with the strategic outlook of the German Chancellor, Willy Brandt, who was simultaneously opening to the Soviet bloc with the *détente* of *Ostpolitik* and binding Germany into the West with his plans for enlargement and monetary union.

However, economic and monetary union would have to wait, as German desire for strong coordination of economic policy was a step too far for the French. The result was a system for cooperation on exchange rates that was too weak to survive the international currency turbulence of that period. Similarly, the system devised for foreign policy cooperation was strictly intergovernmental: this limited its impact. While France was able to secure a very favourable financial regulation for CAP, this was balanced by giving the European Parliament the power to share control of the budget with the Council of Ministers, a decision consolidated in treaties in 1970 and 1975. While this was just a foot in the door to budgetary powers for the Parliament, it was to grow into a major element in the EU's institutional structure.

Britain, together with Denmark and Ireland, joined the EEC in January 1973 (Figure 3), while the Norwegians rejected accession in a referendum. The British too were to vote in a referendum in 1975. Harold Wilson had replaced Edward Heath as Prime Minister in 1974 following an election victory by the Labour Party, which was turning more and more against the EEC (a position that lasted into the 1980s). After a somewhat cosmetic 'renegotiation', the Wilson government did recommend continued membership; and in 1975 the voters approved it by a two-to-one majority. With Margaret Thatcher's Conservatives coming to power in 1979, a new line of tension was opened, as she fought to 'get our money back', as she put it, by blocking much EEC business until she secured agreement in 1984 to reduce Britain's high net contribution to the EEC's budget.

As so often in the EU's history, the 1970s saw the simultaneous development of both intergovernmental and supranational activities. French President Valéry Giscard d'Estaing, a Gaullist by tradition, launched both regular meetings of the European Council between national leaders and direct elections to the European Parliament. The European Council was soon to play a central part in taking Community decisions, settling conflicts that members of the Council of Ministers were unable to resolve, and agreeing on major package deals. Provision had already been made for direct elections in the treaties of the 1950s, but it was only now that governments agreed and the first elections were held in June 1979. This step towards representative democracy was to have a big impact on the Community's future development.

3. British entry: Heath signs the Treaty of Accession.

Of similar importance, 1979 also saw the creation of a system of exchange rate stabilization—the European Monetary System (EMS)—which was to shape later discussions on monetary union.

Single market, Draft Treaty on European Union, and southern enlargement

Jacques Delors became President of the Commission in January 1985 (Figure 4). He had visited each member state to find out what major project was likely to be accepted by all of them. As a federalist in Monnet's tradition, his short-list contained projects—single market, single currency, common defence policy, and institutional reform—that could be seen as steps in a federal direction. But Thatcher, whose view of federalism was akin to de Gaulle's, and so was hostile to the currency, defence, and institutional projects, was at the same time a militant economic liberal who saw the single market as an important measure of trade liberalization. European economies had lost momentum during the hard times of the 1970s and all the governments

4. Delors: single market, single currency, single-minded European.

accepted the single market project as a way to break out of what was then called 'eurosclerosis'. The project was strongly backed by the more dynamic firms and the main business associations, especially since the Luxembourg 'compromise' had served to let non-tariff barriers to trade build up during the period.

The successful abolition of tariffs on internal trade had demonstrated the value of a programme with a timetable. So the Commission produced a list of some 300 measures to be enacted by the end of 1992 in order to complete the single market by removing the non-tariff barriers. The Commissioner in charge of the project was Lord Cockfield, a former minister in the Thatcher government; and the programme was rapidly drafted in time to be presented to the European Council in Milan in June 1985.

Meanwhile the European Parliament had prepared a political project: a Draft Treaty on the European Union, inspired by Altiero Spinelli, the leading figure since the 1950s among those federalists who saw the drafting of a constitution as the royal road to federation. The Draft Treaty was designed to reform the Community's institutions so as to give them a federal character; to extend its powers to include most of those that would be normal in a federation, with the key exception of defence; and to come into effect when ratified by a majority of the member states, with suitable arrangements to be negotiated with any states that did not ratify. While there was widespread support for the draft in most of the founder states, the German government was among those that were not prepared to countenance the probable exclusion of Britain. President Mitterrand did, however, express support for the draft, albeit in somewhat equivocal terms; and its main proposals were presented to the European Council in Milan along with the Commission's single market project.

The European Council decided to convene an Intergovernmental Conference (IGC) on treaty amendment, overriding British, Danish, and Greek opposition with its first ever use of a majority vote.

The IGC considered amendments relating not only to the single market programme but also to a number of the proposals in the Parliament's Draft Treaty. The outcome was the Single European Act, which provided for completion of the single market by 1992; gave the EC competences in the fields of the environment, technological research and development, social policies relating to employment, and 'cohesion'; and brought the foreign policy cooperation into the EC's treaty architecture (albeit with the retention of distinct intergovernmental procedures)—hence the title 'Single European Act', to distinguish it from a proposal to keep foreign policy separate. The Single Act also provided for qualified majority voting in a number of areas of single market legislation, and the strengthening of the European Parliament through a 'cooperation procedure' which gave it influence over such legislation, together with a procedure requiring its assent to treaties of association and accession.

The EEC was enlarged in 1981 to include Greece and, in 1986, Portugal and Spain. All three had been ruled by authoritarian regimes and saw the Community as a support for their democracies as well as for economic modernization. The EEC for its part wanted them to be viable member states and to be supportive of its projects, such as the single market. It was to this end that the cohesion policy, based on a doubling of the structural funds for assisting the development of economically weaker regions, was included in the Single Act.

Thus the Single Act strengthened both the Community's powers and its institutions, with influence from a combination of governments, economic interests, social concerns, the Commission, the Parliament, and a variety of federalist forces. It was succeeded by the Maastricht, Amsterdam, and Nice Treaties, likewise strengthening both powers and institutions, and responding to similar combinations of pressures. This would not have happened had the Single Act not been successful. But the prospect of the single market helped to revive the economy, and the EC institutions gained in strength as they dealt with the vast programme of legislation.

Spinelli died a few weeks after the signing of the Single Act under the impression that it was a failure: 'a dead mouse', as he put it (Figure 5). In fact, it initiated a relaunching of the Community which may have been as far-reaching in its effects as that which led to the Treaties of Rome.

5. Today's European leaders remember Altiero Spinelli at Ventotene, August 2016.

Maastricht and Amsterdam Treaties, and enlargement from twelve to fifteen

Following his success with the single market, Delors was determined to pursue the project of a single currency. Thatcher had not been alone in opposing it. Most Germans, proud of the Deutschmark as representing the EC's strongest currency, were decidedly unenthusiastic. But it remained a major French objective, for economic as well as political reasons; and Helmut Kohl, a long-standing federalist, held that it would be a crucial step towards a federal Europe. While he facilitated the preparation of plans for the single currency, however, he faced difficulty in securing the necessary support in Germany.

The events of 1989 were a seismic upheaval. With the disintegration of the Soviet bloc, which opened up the prospect of enlarging the EC to the East, German unification also became possible. But Kohl needed Mitterrand's support: both for formal reasons because France, as an occupying power, had the right to veto German unification; and, pursuing the policy initiated by Brandt, to ensure that new eastern relationships did not undermine the EC and the Franco-German partnership. Mitterrand saw the single currency as the way to anchor Germany irrevocably in the EC system, and hence as a condition for German unification; and this ensured for Kohl the necessary support in Germany to proceed with the project (Map 1).

The result was the Maastricht Treaty, which provided not only for the euro and the European Central Bank but also for other competences and institutional reforms. The organization was given some powers in the fields of education, youth, culture, and public health. Its institutions were strengthened in a number of ways, including more scope for qualified majority voting in the Council of Ministers. The role of the European Parliament was enhanced through a 'co-decision' procedure that required its

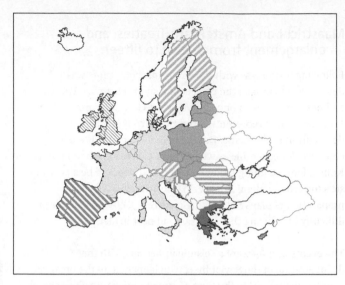

☐ **1957** (Belgium, France, Germany (West), Italy, Luxembourg, The Netherlands)

▨ **1973** (Denmark, Ireland, the United Kingdom)

■ **1981** (Greece)

▨ **1986** (Portugal, Spain)

▨ **1995** (Austria, Finland, Sweden)

■ **2004** (Cyprus, Czech Republic, Estonia, Hungary, Latvia, Lithuania, Malta, Poland, Slovakia, Slovenia)

▤ **2007** (Bulgaria, Romania)

▥ **2013** (Croatia)

Map 1. The changing membership of the EU since 1957.

approval as well as that of the Council of Ministers for laws in a number of fields; and it secured the right to approve—or not—the appointment of each new Commission. Two new 'pillars' were set up alongside the EC: one for a 'common foreign and security policy'; the other relating to freedom of movement and internal security, for what was called 'cooperation in justice and home affairs'—renamed in the Amsterdam Treaty as 'police and judicial cooperation in criminal matters'. The basis for both was intergovernmental, though they were related to the EC institutions. The whole unwieldy structure was named the EU, with the first, central, EC pillar as well as the other two.

Although John Major had succeeded Mrs Thatcher as Prime Minister with the avowed intention of moving to 'the heart of Europe', he insisted that Britain would participate neither in the single currency nor in a 'social chapter' on matters relating to employment. In order to secure agreement on the treaty as a whole, it was accepted that Britain could opt out of both, together with Denmark as far as the single currency was concerned.

The Maastricht Treaty was signed in February 1992 and entered into force in November 1993 after a number of vicissitudes: two Danish referendums, in the first of which it was rejected and in the second approved after some small adjustments had been made; a French referendum in which the voters accepted it by a tiny majority; in London, a fraught ratification process in the House of Commons; and in Germany, a lengthy deliberation by the Constitutional Court before it rejected a claim that the treaty was unconstitutional. These episodes, together with evidence that citizens' approval of the EU was declining in most member states, seemed alarming, particularly to people of federalist orientation.

The more federalist among the governments, however, felt that the Maastricht Treaty did not go far enough. With the decisive new monetary powers and the prospect of further enlargement, they wanted to make the EU more effective and democratic. By the time the Treaty entered into force, accession negotiations with Austria, Finland, and Sweden had already begun, and Cyprus, Malta, Norway, and Switzerland had lodged their applications. Norway negotiated an accession treaty but it was again rejected in a referendum; and the Swiss government withdrew its application after defeat in a referendum on the much looser European Economic Area (EEA). Negotiations with Cyprus and Malta were to begin in 1998 and 2001 at the same times as those with ten Central and Eastern European states, following the European Council's decision that the latter could join when they fulfilled the economic and political conditions. But Austria, Finland, and Sweden acceded in 1995. So the Maastricht Treaty was followed in 1996 by another IGC, from which emerged the Amsterdam Treaty, signed in 1997 and in force in 1999.

The Amsterdam Treaty revisited a number of EU competences, including those relating to the two intergovernmental pillars. A new chapter on employment was added to the Treaty on European Union (TEU) reflecting concern about the unemployment that had persisted through the 1990s at around the 10 per cent level, together with fears that it might be aggravated if the European Central Bank were to pursue a tight money policy.

Among the institutions, the European Parliament gained most, with co-decision extended to include the majority of legislative decisions, and the right of approval over the appointment not only of the Commission as a whole but before that, of its president. Since the president, once approved, was given the right to accept or reject the nominations for the other members of the Commission, the Parliament's power over the Commission was considerably enhanced. Its part in the process that led to the Commission's resignation in March 1999 and in the appointment of the new Commission demonstrated the significance of parliamentary control over the executive. The treaty also gave the Commission's president more power over the other commissioners.

At the same time as adding these federal elements to the institutions, the Amsterdam Treaty reflected fears that the EU would not be able to meet the challenges ahead if new developments were to be inhibited by the unanimity procedure. This led to a procedure of 'enhanced cooperation', allowing a group of member states to proceed with a project in which a minority did not wish to participate, a procedure that only rarely has been used since. Six weeks before the meeting of the European Council in Amsterdam that reached agreement on the treaty, Tony Blair became Prime Minister following Labour's election victory. The new British government adopted the social chapter and, expressing a more favourable attitude towards the EU, accepted without demur such reforms as the increase in EU Parliament powers. But Britain, along with Denmark and Ireland, did opt out of the provision to abolish frontier controls along with only partial transfer of the related cooperation in justice and home affairs to the EC pillar—even if the British government did later cooperate quite energetically in that field. As regards external security, Europe's weak performance in former Yugoslavia had spurred demands for a stronger defence capacity; and Britain both accepted provision for this in the Amsterdam Treaty and then joined with France to initiate action along these lines.

Enlargement to twenty-eight, constitutionalization, and Lisbon

Following their emergence from Soviet domination, ten Central and Eastern European states obtained association with the EU, and then sought accession. They faced an enormous task of transforming their economies and polities from that of centralized communist control to the market economies and pluralist democracies that membership required. But by 1997 the EU judged that five of them had made enough progress to justify starting accession negotiations in the following year; and negotiations with another five opened in January 2000. By 2004, accession was completed for the Czech Republic, Estonia,

Hungary, Latvia, Lithuania, Poland, Slovakia, and Slovenia, together with Cyprus and Malta; and Bulgaria and Romania joined in 2007. Turkey's candidature was also recognized; but while negotiations were opened 2005 they have been shelved for the foreseeable future.

With such a formidable enlargement ahead, the question of deepening arose again. Reform of some policies was necessary, in particular for agriculture and the structural funds. The Commission's proposals for this, entitled 'Agenda 2000', were partially adopted, though further measures were required. As regards reform of the institutions, another IGC was convened in 2000, leading to the Nice Treaty which was signed in 2001 and in force in 2002.

The result was an inadequate response to the prospect of nearly doubling the number of member states. It introduced modest increases in the scope of qualified majority voting in the Council of Ministers and of legislative co-decision with the Parliament, as well as some procedural improvements for the Court of Justice. It addressed the growth in the number of Commissioners accompanying enlargement by further enhancing the power of the president over commissioners and by taking some steps to limit their number. It also saw the 'solemn proclamation' of the Charter of Fundamental Rights, as a means of strengthening the EU's provisions in this field. But the weighting of votes in the Council of Ministers and the number of members of the European Parliament (MEPs) for each state became the subject of unprincipled horse-trading. The German and Italian governments found the treaty so unsatisfactory that they proposed a 'deeper and wider debate about the future of the Union'; and the European Council in December 2001, under Belgian presidency, decided to establish a convention to make further proposals to an IGC in 2004.

The Laeken Declaration, named after the Brussels suburb where the European Council met, was cleverly crafted to secure unanimous agreement by including, in what amounted to terms of reference for the Convention, items aimed at the more intergovernmentalist as well as the more federalist members. So the Convention met in February 2002 with a very broad remit, and its 105 members covered a wide spectrum of political orientations, with two MEPs representing each of the then twenty-seven member and candidate states plus Turkey as a forthcoming candidate, sixteen MEPs, one representative of each government, two members of the European Commission, a president, and two vice-presidents.

The President of the Convention, former French President Valéry Giscard d'Estaing, steered a course between federalism and intergovernmentalism. The majority of its members, including MEPs, preferred a more federal than intergovernmental orientation; and Giscard satisfied them by favouring elements of federal reform within the EC pillar. But the amended EU Treaty drafted by the Convention would not be unanimously accepted by the ensuing IGC if the federal elements intruded too far into the fields of common foreign and security policy, and macroeconomic policy. Nor would some of the representatives of heads of government in the Convention have accepted the consensus that Giscard sought as the outcome of its work; indeed, Giscard himself may well have sympathized with this view. So he steered the Convention towards more intergovernmental proposals in those fields. In July 2003, it acclaimed a consensus on a draft Constitution. Its main thrust was towards more effective and democratic institutions, while also tidying up much of the existing TEC provisions for common policies and providing a basis for further development of a common defence. The IGC was convened in October 2003; agreed some amendments in an intergovernmental direction; and concluded a year later when all the member and acceding states signed the treaty establishing a Constitution for Europe. Eighteen of them ratified the treaty, but it was rejected by substantial majorities in French and Dutch referendums in 2005.

It can be read as a mark of the condition of the integration process that despite the populations of two founding member states being unwilling to approve a more explicitly constitutional grounding for the EU, there was still a desire to persist on the part of their governments, albeit after a 'period of reflection'. The continuing mismatch between elite and popular engagement with the EU since Maastricht was doubtless exacerbated by the former's unwillingness to generate debate about what is too often dismissed as remote or complex. Certainly, the revival of the large majority of the Constitutional Treaty's contents with a brief IGC in 2007 and a ratification that almost completely sidestepped ratification referendums did little to endear the EU to the public. This was borne out by a 'no' vote in Ireland (the one country to hold such a referendum), and legal challenges in Germany and the Czech Republic, all of which meant that the final document, the Treaty of Lisbon, only came into force in December 2009.

Despite being the end result of such a fundamental review of the EU's legal basis and of almost a decade's worth of debate, the Lisbon Treaty looks a lot like its predecessors. It retains the basic mix of intergovernmental and federal elements, keeps member states in a privileged position of decision-making, and keeps many competences where they previously were to be found. However, it does mark a new stage in the EU's development.

Most importantly, Lisbon ended the pillar system, pulling all of the remnants of the second and third pillars into the first, which was governed by the renamed Treaty on the Functioning of the EU (TFEU). The TEU remained to provide a wider framework and legal personality for the EU, as well as space for the Charter of Fundamental Rights to gain legal status in underpinning the EU's activities. Voting in the Council of Ministers was simplified, while the Parliament further extended its legislative power, with the Ordinary Legislative Procedure (OLP) applying to most activities, and with a final say on all areas of spending. The European

Council acquired a permanent president, to chair and represent it, replacing the rotating presidency, which was now confined to the Council of Ministers. The treaty further consolidated external representation, by creating a high representative for foreign affairs, who would be simultaneously a vice-president of the Commission and chair of the Foreign Affairs Council. Importantly, formal roles were given to national parliaments to challenge legislative proposals, and to European citizens to submit petitions for action by the Commission.

For many, the Lisbon Treaty represented the end of an era of constitutionalization in EU affairs. However, the rapid deterioration of the global economy from 2007, which was to take up much more of European politicians' attention in the years that followed, has highlighted the need for a continued debate. The initial financial crisis, triggered by a collapse in banks' solvency, hit European economies hard, breaking a long period of growth. To this was added (from 2009) a sovereign-debt crisis specific to the Eurozone.

We discuss this further in Chapter 4, but here we would note that despite the varied causes of the sovereign-debt crisis, these were all compounded by the incomplete nature of the Eurozone's integration. Without the capacity to generate Eurozone-wide fiscal transfers or debt creation, global financial markets were able to force governments into repeated rounds of crisis management and intervention, most obviously with the case of Greece. Even the reforms of 2010–12 did not provide a comprehensive resolution, but rather a stop-gap as the Eurozone began a slow and hesitant recovery.

More than anything, the Eurozone crisis called into question the benefits of integration for many and laid the groundwork for increasing disillusionment from publics. This was further shaped by the emergence of a migrant crisis from 2015, as significant numbers of asylum seekers and refugees sought to make their way from conflicts in Syria and elsewhere in the Middle East, crossing the Mediterranean in perilous circumstances and overwhelming the capacity of member states to handle them.

This crisis was compounded by disagreements between members about the appropriate response, at a time when fears of Islamic fundamentalist terrorism were further encouraging support for populist politicians across the EU. As some countries reinstated their border controls, despite their obligations on free movement of people, others—notably Germany and Sweden—welcomed those who arrived. Even the partial resolution of the situation with an agreement with Turkey to provide local facilities highlighted the difficulty of deciding EU policy in a way that balanced the differing priorities of security, humanity, and effectiveness.

All of this played into the long-standing debate in the UK about its relationship with the EU. David Cameron's 2013 promise to hold a referendum on membership had seemed—at the time—to be an empty letter, but his unexpected formation of a single-party government two years later forced him onto a path for which he had little prepared. There was an attempt to renegotiate terms with the EU, resulting in as much flexibility as was possible within the framework of the treaties to restrict free movement of people, but this was far from what Cameron had claimed to have sought from the process. Faced with a diverse set of opponents who used the tempting, if vague, notion of 'taking back control', Cameron was unable to articulate a convincing narrative about the value of membership, and lost the ensuing referendum in June 2016. That it was to take another nine months before the UK could submit its formal notification to leave was a mark not only of the lack of preparation for such an eventuality by the British government, but also of the complexity of the task it now faces.

We conclude here by noting that the problems facing the EU in recent years have been uneven and varied, occurring at the same time that more countries joined the EU—for example, Croatia in 2013—and the euro itself. But this is not to say those problems have been insignificant: from the British referendum to the seeming wave of populist parties across the EU, the question of what future there might be for the organization is now more open than ever before.

Chapter 3
How the EU is governed

The EU has major economic and environmental powers, and is increasingly active in foreign policy, defence, and internal security. It uses these powers through a number of institutions that allow it to formulate and decide upon policy as well as to arbitrate disputes between the different parts of the organization (see Figure 6). But how is its power used and controlled? How is the EU governed?

The answer, according to many intergovernmentalists, is through cooperation between the governments of member states: the other institutions are peripheral to the Council of Ministers in which the governments are represented, and this fact will not go away. But while the Council of Ministers is still the most powerful institution, federalists regard the Parliament, Commission, and Court of Justice not only as sufficiently independent of the states to have changed the nature of the relationships among them, but also as major actors in a process that may, and should, result in the EU becoming a federal polity.

The European Council and the Council of Ministers

The Council of Ministers consists of ministers representing the member states; and at the highest level there is the European

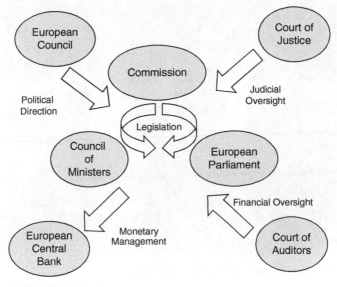

6. The EU's institutions.

Council of heads of state or government together with the president of the European Council and president of the European Commission. Heads of state are included in the title because several presidents participate as well as their prime ministers, since they have some of the functions performed by heads of government elsewhere.

The European Council meets three or four times a year (Figure 7) and takes decisions that require resolution or impulsion at that political level, sometimes because ministers have been unable to resolve an issue in the Council of Ministers, sometimes because a package deal involving many subjects, such as a major amending treaty or a seven-year financial perspective, has to be assembled. The European Council also has to 'define general political guidelines'. Its rotating presidency is an important function, both for the management of current business and for launching new projects.

7. European Council 1979: facing different ways.

The president of the European Council is the closest that the EU
has come to a national equivalent, representing the EU externally
and providing a focus to the European Council's work. Its
incumbents have focused primarily on the managerial aspect of
the post, helping to coordinate the response to the Eurozone crisis,
and establishing a *modus vivendi* with the other institutions, most
notably the Commission.

The meetings themselves are confined to two EU presidents (of
the European Council and the Commission) and the twenty-eight
heads of state and government, and usually the EU's high
representative for foreign affairs. Outside the meeting room, they
are surrounded by a vast media circus which presents the results
to the citizens of different countries in radically different ways,
with each leader seeking to make the best possible impression
on their respective constituencies.

The 'Presidency Conclusions' are issued after each meeting, usually in a lengthy document, sometimes with bulky annexes. The European Council itself initiates only a few of their decisions, and does not have time for thorough discussion of all that is put before it, especially when dealing with technical briefs, as in the Eurozone crisis. More typically, most of the detail and the 'political guidelines' emerge from the EU's institutions, working with the European Council's president.

The Council of Ministers is a more complicated body. Which minister attends a given meeting depends on its subject. It meets in approximately ten forms, including an Economic and Financial Council (Ecofin), an Agriculture Council, a Foreign Affairs Council (under the chair of the high representative), and a General Affairs Council comprising the foreign ministers, which is supposed to coordinate the work of the other councils, but is in practice hard put to control councils of ministers from powerful departments of state. Each council is chaired by the representative of the state that is serving (they take it in turn for a term of six months each) as president-in-office.

Unlike the European Council, large numbers attend the meetings of the Council of Ministers. Several officials as well as ministers (or their representatives) from each member state are present; and they are joined by the relevant commissioners. Officials from the Commission also attend, as well as those from the Council Secretariat, which provides continuity from one presidency to the next and has become quite a powerful institution. Also unlike the European Council, much of the Council of Ministers' work is legislative and some is executive.

After protracted pressure the Council of Ministers now holds its legislative sessions in public, but its proceedings remain more like negotiations in a diplomatic conference than a debate in a normal democratic legislature.

The resemblance to an international negotiation was yet more pronounced before the mid-1980s when, with the launching of the single market programme, qualified majority voting (QMV) began to replace unanimity as the procedure for legislative decisions. Though the treaty stipulated that only texts proposed by the Commission could be made into law, the unanimity procedure gave each minister a veto with which to pressurize the Commission into amending a proposal; and although the treaty provided for QMV on a range of subjects, the veto implicit in the Luxembourg 'compromise' extended its scope in practice to virtually the whole of legislation. The Committee of Permanent Representatives of the member states (called Coreper, after its French acronym) seeks common ground beforehand in the governments' reactions to the Commission's proposals; and given the difficulty of securing unanimity, it was thanks to the dedication of many of these officials that the EU was able to function at all. But measures identified by the Commission as being in the general interest and enjoying the support of a large majority were often reduced to a 'lowest common denominator', reached after long delay.

This contributed to the failure to make much progress towards the single market until the voting procedures were changed following the Single European Act. Up until then, single market measures had been passed at a rate of about one a month, barely enough to keep up with new developments in the economy, let alone to complete the whole programme inside a quarter of a century. But the Single Act's provision for QMV on most of the single market legislation helped speed the rate to about one a week, putting the bulk of the laws in place by 1992.

The system for QMV has undergone several iterations and the reader is probably as grateful as the authors that he or she is now spared the more complex versions! The version introduced by Lisbon requires 55 per cent of states and 65 per cent of population to reach the threshold: this decouples the system from the previous squabbles over voting weights, while protecting both large and small states from being structurally marginalized.

While QMV is designed to ensure that laws wanted by a substantial majority can be passed, the Council of Ministers still tries to avoid overriding a minority of one government about something the latter regards as important. This is due partly to the need to treat minorities with care in a diverse polity, and that motive has an edge in the EU, where a disgruntled member government could retaliate by bringing business to a halt on other matters still subject to unanimity. Partly it reflects the diplomatic culture which prevails in the Council of Ministers. But unlike the Luxembourg 'compromise', votes are quite often taken, and proceedings take place in 'the shadow of the vote', so that ministers prefer to compromise than to run the risk that a vote will produce an outcome which is worse for them. Often the president, judging that a problem has been resolved, suggests that a consensus has been reached and, if there is no dissent, the Council of Ministers accepts the text without a formal vote.

With the use of QMV for single market legislation, the Luxembourg veto began to fade away, so that QMV became the context for a wider range of decisions; and it was extended by the successive treaties to cover almost all fields of legislation. The remaining handful to which unanimity applies come under a variety of headings. These typically relate to structural issues, such as membership of the EU, enhanced cooperation and citizenship, or to policy areas of particular sensitivity. Most notably for the daily operation of the EU, much of foreign policy has retained unanimity, as discussed in Chapter 8. Obviously, the greater the number of member states, the harder it becomes to reach unanimous agreement. So pressure has always existed to reduce the scope for the unanimity procedure and this has been a source of conflict between those with a more, or less, federalist orientation. A similar argument arises about the Council of Ministers' executive role.

Unlike a legislative body in most democracies, the Council of Ministers exercises significant executive powers. Although the Commission is, as Monnet envisaged, the EU's principal executive body, the treaty allows the Council of Ministers to 'impose requirements' on the way in which the Commission implements the laws, or even to see to their implementation itself. This used to happen under a complex system known as 'comitology', where individual committees of member state officials supervised implementation of particular pieces of legislation. While some oversight was possible by the Commission and Parliament, the scope for obstruction and delay led to its partial replacement at Lisbon by a new 'delegated acts' process, which removes these committees for certain legislation, and the renaming of comitology as 'implementing acts'. However, this new system remains deeply opaque, not least because it is at the discretion of the legislators to decide which system to use. Certainly, the long-standing concerns about the transparency of this part of the legislative process will continue for many years yet.

The European Parliament

MEPs are directly elected by citizens throughout the EU in June of every fifth year. There are 751 of them, distributed among the member states in proportions that favour the smaller states, though to a lesser degree than in the weighting of votes in the Council of Ministers: ranging from ninety-six from Germany; over seventy each from France, Italy, and the UK; over fifty each from Poland and Spain; down to six each from Cyprus, Estonia, Luxembourg, and Malta (see Chart 1).

The political culture of the European Parliament differs radically from that of the Council of Ministers. The meetings are open to the public; voting by simple majority is the routine; and the MEPs usually vote by party group rather than by state. Roughly two-thirds of the MEPs elected in June 2014 belong to centrist party groups, with the centre-right Christian Democrat and Conservative EPP

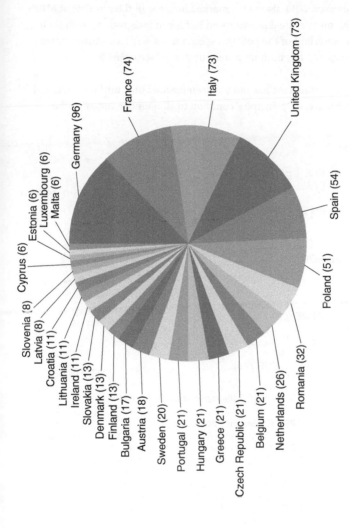

Chart 1. Number of MEPs from each state, 2017.

Germany (96)
France (74)
Italy (73)
United Kingdom (73)
Spain (54)
Poland (51)
Romania (32)
Netherlands (26)
Belgium (21)
Czech Republic (21)
Greece (21)
Hungary (21)
Portugal (21)
Sweden (20)
Austria (18)
Bulgaria (17)
Denmark (13)
Finland (13)
Slovakia (13)
Ireland (11)
Lithuania (11)
Croatia (11)
Latvia (8)
Slovenia (8)
Cyprus (6)
Estonia (6)
Luxembourg (6)
Malta (6)

(European People's Party) and the centre-left S&D (Progressive Alliance of Socialists and Democrats) by far the largest groupings. However, 2014 also saw a marked increase in the number of MEPs with more critical positions on European integration, from both left and right of the political spectrum, as well as a Conservative group that has built up much substance (see Chart 2).

While agreement has not yet been reached on a uniform electoral procedure, or 'principles common to all member states' as the

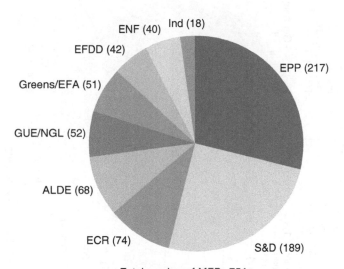

Total number of MEPs 751

EPP	European People's Party
S&D	Progressive Alliance of Socialists and Democrats
ALDE	Alliance of Liberals and Democrats for Europe
ECR	European Conservatives and Reformists
GUE/NGL	European United Left/Nordic Green Left
Greens/EFA	The Greens/European Free Alliance
EFDD	Europe of Freedom and Direct Democracy
ENF	Europe of Nations and Freedom
Ind	Independent

Chart 2. Party groups in the Parliament in 2017.

Amsterdam Treaty more tolerantly put it, all the states now operate systems of proportional representation. The balance between the mainstream parties has otherwise been fairly stable, with neither the centre-right nor the centre-left able to command a majority alone. Hence broad coalitions across the centre are needed to ensure a majority for voting on legislation or the budget; and this is all the more necessary for amending or rejecting measures under the increasingly important co-decision procedure, where an absolute majority of 376 votes is required. The well-developed system of committees, each preparing the Parliament's positions and grilling the Commissioners in a field of the EU's activities, also tends to encourage consensual behaviour. But there has none the less been a sharper left–right division since the elections of 1999, when the centre-right became structurally larger than the centre-left, a pattern reinforced by enlargement.

Although the Parliament has performed well enough in using its now considerable powers over legislation and the budget, the voters' turnout has declined with each election, from 63 per cent in 1979 to 43 per cent in 2014. One reason is a general trend of declining turnouts in elections within member states. Another is a widespread decline in support for the EU. Yet another may be that the Parliament in particular has been exposed to critical and, particularly in Britain, downright hostile media comment, fastening on matters such as the prolonged failure to establish an adequate system for controlling MEPs' expenses (largely the fault of MEPs themselves), and the two costly buildings in Brussels and Strasbourg between which it commutes (entirely the fault of governments). Citizens, moreover, remain largely ignorant of what the Parliament is and can do.

The legislative role has developed from mere consultation at first, through the cooperation procedure initiated by the Single Act, to the co-decision introduced by the Maastricht Treaty and extended through to Lisbon to the point where it now applies to the large majority of legislation, under its new name of the 'Ordinary

Legislative Procedure' (Figure 8). In addition, Lisbon also gives the Parliament equal rights to agree the entire budget with the Council of Ministers, allowing it to provide oversight into areas such as agriculture that had previously been shielded.

While the Parliament's share of power to determine the budget is an essential element of democratic control, its role in supervising how the money is spent has had the greatest impact. As well as its power of scrutiny over the Commission's administrative and financial activities, the Parliament has the right to grant 'discharge': to approve—or not—the Commission's implementation of the previous year's budget, on the basis of a report from the Court of Auditors. If not satisfied, the Parliament withholds discharge until the Commission has undertaken to do what is required. Thus in 1998, after the Parliament had withheld discharge for the 1996 accounts and was not satisfied with the Commission's response, it appointed a high-level expert committee to investigate in more detail. They produced a devastating report on mismanagement and

8. **Elected representatives at work: European Parliament sitting.**

some cases of corruption; and the Commission, anticipating the Parliament's use of its power of dismissal, resigned in March 1999.

Having demonstrated its powers over both appointment and dismissal of the Commission, the Parliament has since used its influence to secure the appointment of a candidate for Commission president who reflects the results of European elections. This was seen in 2014, when each group in the European Parliament put forward a *Spitzenkandidat* or 'lead candidate', on the understanding that the Parliament would only support as Commission president that candidate nominated by the grouping with the most support in the Parliament after the election.

The Parliament shares power equally with the Council of Ministers for most legislation and all of the budget; and it has proved much better able than the Council of Ministers to control the Commission. So it can be said that the Parliament is more than halfway towards fulfilling the functions of enacting legislation and controlling the executive, which a house of the citizens in a federal legislature would perform. The Council of Ministers for its part would be akin to a house of the states, save that the unanimity procedure still applies to some legislation, only its legislative sessions are held in public, and it has retained executive powers that ill accord with its legislative role.

The European Commission

While the Commission, as it stands today, is not the federal executive that Monnet envisaged, it is, with its right of 'legislative initiative', its functions in executing EU policies, and as 'watchdog of the Treaty', a great deal more than the secretariat of an international organization.

The Treaty of Rome gave the Commission the principal right of legislative initiative, that is, to propose the texts for laws to the

Parliament and the Council of Ministers. The aim was to ensure that the laws would be based more on a view of the general interest of the Community and its citizens than would result from initiatives of the member state governments, and that there would be more coherence in the legislative programme than they or the councils with their various functional responsibilities could provide. Armed with this power, the Commission was in its early days often called the 'motor of the Community', although this became much less the case following the Empty Chair Crisis of the 1960s. Even where leadership did emerge subsequently—as with the 'Delors package' of budgetary reform in 1992, and potentially with the 2017 White Paper on the future of Europe—this has also been buoyed up with help from member states.

The Commission has also been called the 'watchdog' because it has to ensure that the EU's treaties and laws are applied, notably by member states. If it has evidence of an infringement, it has to issue a 'reasoned opinion' to the state in question. Should the latter then fail to comply, the Commission can take it to the Court of Justice. This is what happened in 2002 when the French government refused to accept restrictions on fishing designed to protect overstressed stocks. The Court of Justice found against France, which continued to allow this to happen, resulting in a second case in 2005, where the Court of Justice imposed fines in excess of €77 million. The Commission is also responsible for executing EU law and policy, though much of it is delegated to member state governments and other agencies.

In order to ensure that the Commission works in the general interest of the EU, the treaty requires that its independence of any outside interests be 'beyond doubt'; and the commissioners, on taking up office, have to make a 'solemn undertaking' to that effect. Although the treaty provides for their nomination by 'common accord' among the governments, each government has in the past made its own nomination and this has been accepted by the others. But this can no longer be taken for granted, because the accord of the Commission's newly appointed president is now also required before the Parliament's approval of the Commission as a whole.

Until 2005 there were two commissioners from each of the larger and one from each of the smaller states. But the impending enlargement caused concern that a larger Commission would be less effective, so the Nice Treaty limited the number of commissioners, as from 2005, to one from each member state. Proposals for an even smaller number were stoutly resisted by smaller states and the initial rejection of the Lisbon Treaty by Irish voters in 2008 resulted in agreement that the current system should remain.

Reducing the number of commissioners to fewer than one per state is by no means the only way to secure effectiveness. The top tier of governments, such as the British Cabinet, usually has over twenty members, in some cases over thirty; and this has worked because a prime minister has the power to control the other members. Treaties since Amsterdam have moved the Commission some way in that direction by giving the president the power not only to share in the decisions to nominate the other commissioners, but also to exercise 'political guidance' over the commissioners, to allocate and 'reshuffle' their responsibilities, to appoint vice-presidents, and to sack a commissioner (Figure 9). The presence of the EU's high representative for foreign policy as a vice-president since Lisbon has also helped to provide management of policy coordination, both internally and externally.

In treaty terminology, the Commission is the whole body of commissioners. In common usage, it also refers to the Commission's staff. But it is usually clear whether reference is being made to the commissioners or the Commission's 30,000 employees; and despite loose talk of a bloated bureaucracy, this is roughly the same number employed by a European city.

9. The Juncker Commission meets after its appointment in 2014.

Since QMV now applies to the bulk of legislation, the Commission's sole right of initiative has given it a strong position in the legislative process. The Council of Ministers can amend the Commission's text, but only by unanimity, which here works in the Commission's favour instead of against it, for while the Commission normally prefers to accommodate governments' wishes, it is better placed to resist their pressure on points it regards as important.

The Commission has grown into its legislative role, managing both the EU's internal processes and an extensive assortment of external interests. But its performance as an executive has been more problematic, not least because execution of policy is largely delegated to the member states. This is a good principle, which works well in Germany's federal system where the Länder administer most of the federal policies. But there the federal government has more power to ensure adequate performance from the Länder, whereas member states tend to resist the

Commission's efforts to supervise them. The answer is surely not more direct administration by Brussels, but rather enough Commission staff to undertake the supervision and stronger powers to ensure proper implementation by the states.

The Commission has a good record in fields such as the administration of competition policy, where it was given the power to do the job itself and has done it well despite a shortage of officials. But there have been serious defects when it has been required to administer expenditure programmes without the staff to do this properly, resulting in defects either in its own work or in that of consultants hired to do it, with sometimes bad and in a few cases fraudulent consequences. This stimulated not only the 1999 resignation, but also the on-going reforms to the administration set out by Neil Kinnock in the early 2000s, aimed at improving recruitment, training, promotion, and audit practices.

Some have argued that the Commission is a European government. How far could this be an accurate description? Within the fields of EU competence, its right of legislative initiative resembles that of a government, and even exceeds it in so far as the Commission's is almost a sole right. But its use of the right is constrained by the Council of Ministers, particularly where the unanimity procedure applies, though also by the use of QMV rather than a simple majority. The difference is, however, greater in comparison with Britain than in those states practising a consensual style of coalition government. The Commission's executive role is constrained by the Council of Ministers and the difficulties of implementation, but it is otherwise not, in principle, far different from that of the German federal government—only the German government has a more effective means of enforcing proper implementation by the Länder. A crucial distinction between the Commission and a government is, indeed, that the Commission does not possess any physical means of enforcement. It has, moreover, only a minor role in general foreign policy, and an even smaller one in defence. Along with the differences, however, there are significant similarities.

The Court of Justice

The rule of law has been key to the success of the EU. Increasingly, in its fields of competence, a framework of law rather than relative power governs the relations between member states, and it applies to their citizens. This establishes 'legal certainty', which is prized by business people because it reduces a major element of risk in their transactions. Politically, it has helped to create the altogether new climate in which war between the states is deemed to be unthinkable.

At the apex of the EU's legal system is the Court of Justice, which the treaties require to ensure that 'in the interpretation and application of the Treaties the law' (taken in a broad sense) 'is observed'.

There is one judge from each member state, appointed for six-year terms by common accord between member states whose independence is to be 'beyond doubt'. The Court of Justice itself judges cases such as those concerning the legality of EU acts, or actions by the Commission against a member state or by one member state against another, alleging failure to fulfil a treaty obligation. But the vast majority of cases involving EU law are those brought by individuals or companies against other such legal persons or governments; and these are tried in the member states' courts, coming before the Court of Justice only if one of those courts asks it to interpret a point of law.

The Court of Justice's most fundamental judgments, delivered in the 1960s, were based on its determination to ensure that the law was observed as the treaty required. The first, on direct effect, provided for individuals to claim their rights under the treaty directly in the states' courts. The second, on the primacy of EU law, was designed to ensure its even application in all the member states; for the rule of law would progressively disintegrate should it be overridden by divergent national laws. Then in 1979 a judgment on the 'Cassis de Dijon' case laid a cornerstone of the single market programme, with the principle of 'mutual recognition' of member states' standards for the safety of products, provided they were judged acceptable; and this radically reduced the need for detailed regulation at the EU level.

The Court of Justice has delivered over 10,000 judgments since its creation, and cases continue to come before it at a rate that makes it hard to reduce the delays of up to eighteen months before judgments can be reached. A subsidiary court—the General Court (formerly the Court of First Instance)—was established to help deal with this problem. It deals with almost all cases brought by individuals or legal persons, relating first and foremost to intellectual property rights, competition policy, and staff disputes. But while this has slowed it has not turned the tide of cases awaiting judgment.

While litigants can appeal from the lower courts, there is no appeal beyond the Court of Justice, which is the final judicial authority on matters within EU competence. To enforce its judgments outside the EU's institutions, however, it depends on the enforcement agencies of the member states. The fact that the large majority of judgments under EU law are made by the states' own courts has instilled the habit of enforcing it; and there has been no refusal to enforce the judgments of the Court of Justice itself, even if there have sometimes been quite long delays before member states have complied with judgments that went against them.

The Court of Justice's jurisdiction is still limited by the treaties, especially in foreign policy. But within these limits, and apart from the almost total reliance on the member states' enforcement agencies, the EU's legal system has largely federal characteristics.

Subsidiarity and flexibility

In a speech delivered in Bruges in 1988, Mrs Thatcher famously evoked the spectre of a 'European super-state exercising a new dominance from Brussels'; and a 'slippery slope' leading towards a 'centralized super-state' has become a favourite metaphor for British eurosceptics. From a different starting point, German Länder have looked askance at proposals for EU competence in fields that belong to them in Germany's federal system. Indeed many federalists find the treaty objective of 'an ever closer union' too open-ended, and most support the principle of 'subsidiarity' as a guide to determine what the EU should do and what it should not do. That principle, which has both Calvinist and Catholic antecedents, requires bodies with responsibilities for larger areas to perform only the functions that those responsible for smaller areas within them cannot do for themselves. Following this principle, the treaty requires the EU to 'take action...only if and insofar as the objective of the proposed action cannot be sufficiently achieved by the Member States', and can, 'by reason of its scale or effects, be better achieved by the Union'.

The Rome Treaty implicitly recognized this principle in distinguishing between two kinds of EU act: the Regulation, which is 'binding in its entirety' on all the member states; and the Directive, which is binding only 'as to the result to be achieved', leaving each state to choose the 'form and methods'. But this was a very partial application of the principle; and Directives were sometimes enacted in such detail as to leave little choice to the states. So the Maastricht Treaty defined subsidiarity and the Amsterdam Treaty laid down detailed procedures aiming to ensure that the principle would be practised by the EU institutions. The inclusion in the Lisbon Treaty of a list of which competences are exclusive to the EU, which are shared with member states, and which are supporting state action has further ensured that there are multiple safeguards against overcentralization.

There are of course disagreements about the fields in which integration is justified. These left their mark on the Maastricht Treaty, in the British opt-outs from the social chapter and the single currency, and those of Denmark on the single currency and defence. Since the treaty can be amended only by unanimity, the other governments had to accept the opting-out if these items were to be included in it; and this led to growing interest in the idea of 'flexibility', enabling those states wanting further integration in a given field to proceed within the EU institutions or, to put it the other way round, allowing a minority to opt out. One purpose was to circumvent the veto of individual member states, whose resistance to reforms might block those most other governments regard as necessary, a concern heightened by inclusion of states that may prove unwilling or unable to proceed with further integration.

The concept of flexibility emerged in the Amsterdam Treaty under the heading of 'enhanced cooperation': a term preferred by federalists because it implied a deeper level of integration among a group of states, whereas eurosceptics tended to see flexibility as a way of loosening bonds in the EU as a whole. The treaties now provide for enhanced cooperation within the EU provided that a number of conditions are met, including that a minimum of nine states be involved at first, agreeing unanimously, and that it remains open to any and all additional states.

Citizens

The concept of citizenship of the EU was introduced in the Maastricht Treaty, which provided that all nationals of the member states are, in addition, also citizens of the EU; and the Amsterdam Treaty added that the two forms of citizenship are complementary. The Maastricht Treaty included a few new rights for the citizens, such as the right to free movement and residence throughout the EU, subject to specified conditions, and the right to vote or stand for election in other member states in local and

European (but not national) elections. This short-list comes on top of specific rights already guaranteed by the treaties, such as protection for member states' citizens against discrimination based on nationality in fields of EU competence, and equal treatment for men and women in matters relating to employment. The EU's institutions are also required to respect fundamental rights, as guaranteed by the European Convention on Human Rights and Fundamental Freedoms. The treaties affirm that the EU is 'founded on the principles of liberty, democracy, respect for human rights and fundamental freedoms, and the rule of law, principles which are common to the member states'; moreover it provides that, in the event of a 'serious and persistent breach' of these principles, a member state can be deprived of some of its rights under the treaty, including voting rights.

In response to concerns that the EU needed to do more to attract the support of its citizens, a 'Charter of Fundamental Rights' was also drafted in 2000 by a convention that set the precedent for the Convention that eventually drafted the Constitutional Treaty. The Lisbon Treaty gave the Charter legal force with regard to the actions of the EU itself, including aspects of the member states' dealings with it. In addition, the treaties provide for the Parliament to appoint an ombudsman to investigate citizens' complaints about maladministration by EU institutions and report the results to Parliament and the institution concerned.

Apart from the question of rights, the system for governing the EU, with its complex mix of intergovernmental and federal elements, makes decision-making difficult, and a satisfactory relationship between the institutions and the citizens hard to achieve. Yet as long as citizens lack the desire to offer the same kind of support for the EU as they do for their own states, electorates could become a centrifugal force leading to disintegration—a risk most vividly demonstrated by the British case. There has been lively academic discussion on the need for EU demos to sustain EU democracy, which has encouraged scepticism regarding its possibility. The EU has, however, been able to benefit from its growing democratic elements such as in the powers of the European Parliament, and that model is still likely to continue, along with the development of the EU as a whole.

Lisbon reaffirmed the need to balance the interests of the EU as a whole and those of member states. The removal of the pillar structure, the strengthening of the European Council with a permanent president, and the integration of foreign policy roles in the person of the high representative offer the potential for a more coherent personality to the EU, although national governments have still sought to hold back common action. Similarly, while national parliaments now have powers to hold up a 'yellow card' to legislative proposals, those parliaments often lack sufficient surveillance mechanisms to make this truly efficient, just as the citizens' initiative whereby a petition with one million signatures can trigger legislative action by the Commission rests on a notion of a European public sphere that is more hope than substance at present. Perhaps just as significantly, Lisbon is the first treaty to provide for an explicit mechanism for a state to withdraw from membership, a mechanism now being used by the UK.

Both Brexit and the continuing debates about economic governance to manage the Eurozone should remind us that the EU reflects the needs of its citizens. These change over time, so it is only right that there should remain an air of contingency over the form of its organization.

Chapter 4
Single market, single currency

While peace among the member states remained at the heart of the Community's purpose, from the second half of the 1950s a large common market became the focus for its action. The strength of the US economy was a striking example of the success of such a market; the Germans and the Dutch wanted liberal trade; and the French accepted the common market in industrial goods provided it was accompanied by the agricultural common market that would favour their own exports.

The idea of a large common market had a dynamic that endured through the subsequent decades, because it reflected the growing reality of economic interdependence. As technologies developed, and with them economies of scale, more and more firms of all sizes needed access to a large, secure market; and for the health of the economy and the benefit of the consumers, the market had to be big enough to provide scope for competition, even among the largest firms. So as the European economies developed, the EEC's original project, centred on abolition of tariffs in a customs union, was succeeded in the 1980s by the single market programme, then in the 1990s by the single currency.

There were both economic and political motives for each of the three projects: the benefits of economic rationality; and the consolidation of the EC system as a framework for peaceful relations among the member states. Economics and politics were also both involved in the substance and outcomes of the projects, because the integration of modern economies requires a framework of law, and hence common political and judicial institutions. Nor would success in either the economic or the political field alone have been enough to sustain the EC. There had to be success in both, which the customs union and the single market each achieved. It was also a combination of economic and political motives that secured the launch of the single currency, though not yet the participation of all member states.

The single market

Tariffs and import quotas were, in the 1950s, still the principal barriers to trade. The international process of reducing them began under American leadership in the Gatt (General Agreement on Tariffs and Trade). But the member states of the EEC wanted to do more. The result was the EEC's customs union, abolishing tariff and quota barriers to their mutual trade, and creating a common external tariff.

Customs union and competition policy

Tariffs and quotas on trade between the member states were removed by stages between 1958 and 1968. Industry responded positively and trade across the frontiers grew even more rapidly than the member states' economies as a whole.

While tariffs and quotas were the main distortions impeding trade, they were not the only impediments. The EC was also given powers to forbid restrictive practices and abuse of dominant positions in the private sector. The Council of Ministers gave the task to the Commission, without intervention by member state governments; and in 1989 the Commission was also given the power to control mergers and acquisitions big enough to pose a threat to competition in the EC. Armed with these powers, the Commission has done much to discourage European-level anti-competitive behaviour and has been seen as the toughest cartel-buster in the world. Thus in 2016, it fined Daimler over €1 billion for illegal market sharing in trucks. Because of the volume of work, the Commission sought to return some of the responsibilities for smaller cases to the member states' competition authorities, leading to a degree of decentralization with the creation of the European Competition Network, in which the Commission and national authorities share information and coordinate investigations.

Unfair competition can also take the form of subsidies given by a member state government to a firm or sector (in EU jargon, 'state aids'), enabling it to undercut efficient competitors and undermine their viability. The Commission has been given the power to forbid such subsidies. But it has been harder to control governments than firms. The Commission has been able to enforce some difficult decisions with reluctant governments; but, especially in the 1970s, after it had been weakened by de Gaulle and with the economies hard hit by recession, it could do little to stem the rising tide of subsidies.

Along with the subsidies, non-tariff barriers proliferated in those years, becoming the main obstacle to trade between member states. One reason was technological progress, generating complex regulations differing from one state to another. More important was pressure for protection from those who were suffering from the prevailing 'stagflation'. The European economy was indeed in bad shape, vividly evoked by the term 'eurosclerosis'. A way out was sought; and the Commission, together with leading business interests, persuaded governments that a programme to complete the EC's internal market was required.

Programme to complete the single market by 1992

With the success of the internal tariff disarmament in the 1960s in mind, some business leaders and members of the Commission's staff worked on the idea of a programme to remove the non-tariff barriers. When Delors became the Commission's President in 1985, he fastened onto this idea as the only major initiative that would be supported by the governments of all the member states: the majority because of its economic merits and the political aim of 'relaunching the Community' after two rather stagnant decades; and Mrs Thatcher because of economic liberalization alone. And, indeed, the latter did the EC the service of nominating the highly capable Lord Cockfield, who had been Trade Minister in her Cabinet, as a commissioner to work with Delors on the project.

Delors and Cockfield put the project to the European Council in June 1985. Whereas the programme for eliminating tariffs in the 1960s could be specified in the treaty in the form of percentage reductions, the removal of non-tariff barriers required a vast programme of EC legislation. Frontier formalities and discrimination resulting from standards and regulations, from public purchasing, and from anomalies in indirect taxation all had to be tackled. The Commission published a White Paper specifying that some 300 measures would have to be enacted and proposing a timetable for completing the programme within eight years. This was approved by the European Council and incorporated in the Single European Act, making completion of the programme by the end of 1992 a treaty obligation.

The removal of non-tariff barriers was already implicit in the Rome Treaty, which prohibited 'all measures having equivalent effect' to import quotas. But because the practice of voting by unanimity had impeded the legislative process, the Single Act provided for qualified majority voting on most of the measures needed to complete the programme. The Commission also reduced the legislative burden by building on the principle of mutual recognition that the Court of Justice had established by its judgment in the Cassis de Dijon case, and by delegating decisions on much of the detail to existing standards institutes. Nevertheless, the single market remained a huge enterprise, surely one of the greatest programmes of legislation liberalizing trade in the history of the world.

It was an outstanding success. The latter half of the 1980s was a period of economic regeneration in the EC. While one cannot be sure how much of that was due to the single market programme, economic research has given it at least some of the credit. The programme certainly contributed to the recovery by generating positive views of business prospects as well as stimulating trade, together with structural reform exemplified by a spate of cross-border mergers. The industrially less well-developed states—Greece, Portugal, and, at that time, Ireland and Spain—fearing they would be damaged by stronger competitors, had secured a doubling of the structural funds to help them adjust; and they too, assisted by this and by the expanding EC economy, benefited from the programme.

Politically, the single market enjoyed a remarkable degree of approval across the spectrum—from federalists to eurosceptics. It has been a classic example of a purpose that is, as the treaty's article on subsidiarity puts it, 'by reason of scale...better achieved by the Community'. The legislative framework has guaranteed producers a very large market and given the consumer a reasonable assurance of competitive behaviour among them. The Commission, Council of Ministers, and Parliament were strengthened by their successful output, comprising the largest part of the vast 'acquis' of EU legislation, decisions, and practices; the value of the Court of Justice as an effective means of unblocking legislation was also cemented.

The programme was largely completed, but significant gaps still remain. The most notable area of difficulties has been in the field of liberalization of services. Despite representing over two-thirds of EU GDP, there is little cross-border provision, not least because of fears in old member states about cheap labour coming from Central and Eastern Europe. This was seen most vividly in the French referendum campaign on the Constitutional Treaty in 2005, when the Bolkestein Directive, which aimed to liberalize services within the EU, became a symbol of social dumping, and the 'Polish plumber' an object of intense political concern. When the Bolkestein Directive was agreed in 2006, it had undergone much modification, weakening its impact.

The single currency

A monetary union requires that money in all its forms can move freely across the frontiers between member states and that changes in exchange rates between them be abolished. The single market programme went far to fulfil the first requirement; and the Exchange Rate Mechanism (ERM) prepared the ground for the second.

The ERM was established in 1979, after an abortive attempt to move to monetary union in the 1970s. It required the central banks to intervene in the currency markets to keep fluctuations in their mutual exchange rates within narrow bands; and by the end of the 1980s it had, with the German Bundesbank as anchor, achieved a strong record of monetary stability. Here again, Britain stood aside at the start, only to then join in 1990, at too high a rate and without the experience of the preceding decade of cooperation. In September 1992, currency turmoil forced the pound out of the ERM on what became known as Black Wednesday, making monetary integration a traumatic subject for many British politicians. The ERM had the opposite effect in other member states, with the benefits of exchange-rate stability flowing to economic operators, and in turn allowing for greater reinvestment in production and new employment, particularly important in a single market.

Almost all governments supported the single currency project, on political grounds even more than economic ones. The most powerful commitment came from France, where a tradition of support for exchange-rate stability was bolstered by the desire to share in the control of a European central bank and thus recover some of the monetary autonomy that had in practice been lost to the Bundesbank. Other member states, apart from Denmark and the UK—both of which secured opt-outs from any commitment to join a single currency—accepted such arguments, especially in the context of a newly unified Germany. For Germany, however, while the political motive for accepting the single currency as a French condition of unification was decisive, there were still reservations about replacing the Deutschmark, with its well-earned strength and stability, by an unproven currency. However, the possibility of building a similar system across the EU was clearly an important motivating factor for an export-driven economy like Germany's; if other states would accept the logic of macroeconomic coordination alongside the currency itself, then this would ultimately serve Germany's interests.

The aim of economic and monetary union

The Maastricht Treaty, in providing for economic and monetary union (Emu), established the European Central Bank (ECB) to be, like the Bundesbank, completely independent. The ECB and the central banks of the member states are together called the European System of Central Banks (ESCB: see Figure 10). The six members of the ECB's Executive Board, together with the governors of the other central banks, comprise the Governing Council of the ECB; and none of these banks, nor any member of their decision-making organs, is to take instructions from any other body. The 'primary objective' of the ESCB is 'to maintain

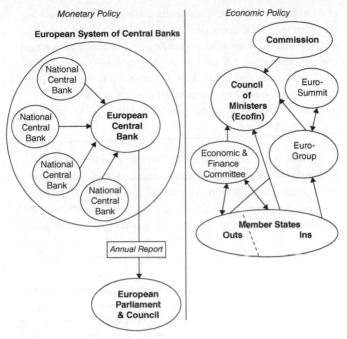

10. Institutions of economic and monetary policy.

price stability' though, subject to that overriding requirement, it
is also to support the EU's 'general economic policies'. The ECB
has the sole right to authorize the issue of notes, and to approve
the quantity of coins issued by the states' mints. In response to
German preference, the single currency was named the 'euro',
rather than the French-sounding 'ecu'.

In order to ensure that only states which had achieved monetary
stability should participate in the euro, five 'convergence criteria'
were established regarding rates of inflation and of interest;
ceilings for budget deficits and for total public debt; and stability
of exchange rates. Budget deficits, for example, were not to exceed
3 per cent of GDP and public debt was to be limited to 60 per cent

of GDP, unless it was 'sufficiently diminishing' and approaching the limit 'at a satisfactory pace'. Only states that had satisfied the criteria were to be allowed to participate; and once again, stages and a timetable were fixed, in order to give at least a minimum number of states the time to do so. Others were to have 'derogations' until they satisfied the criteria, while the British and Danes negotiated opt-outs allowing them to remain outside unless they should choose to join.

In the first stage, all were to accept the ERM, as Britain had briefly done before being ejected by market forces. In the second stage, they were to make enough progress to satisfy the convergence criteria. The third stage began in January 1999 with the 'irrevocable fixing of exchange rates' among the participating states, leading in 2002 to the introduction of the new euro notes and coins which replaced the participants' currencies entirely.

During the mid-1990s, there had been much concern about which countries would be able to achieve the convergence criteria, partly for economic reasons (as with the case of Italy) and partly owing to more political factors relating to the degree of strictness with which the criteria would be interpreted by the EU. In the event, an economic upswing and strong political pressure allowed in eleven of the thirteen states that wanted to join in 1999, with only Greece being specifically excluded (although it was given the green light one year later).

Thus by 2002 the very large majority of member states were Eurozone participants and the issue of relations with those outside became a matter of some concern, because of the binary model of economic policy coordination it required. At least formally, all member states are committed to eventual membership, but in practice a lack of popular support in several countries means that the situation is likely to persist for the foreseeable future.

Newer member states are a case in point. While Slovenia, Malta, Cyprus, Slovakia, Estonia, Latvia, and Lithuania have all joined the Eurozone, a number of other states have reined in some of their initial drive towards participation. Here the factors relate more to the economic flexibility that retaining a national currency allows, rather than any particular sense of the national currency being a strong symbol of national identity. Moreover, all new member states are legally bound to introduce the euro as soon as possible, not having the opt-outs of the UK and Denmark.

A currency in crisis?

If the euro was initially acclaimed as the realization of a new stage in European integration, then recent years have exposed the flipside of this, with the euro as the crucible of political commitment to the EU. The extended period of economic growth in the 2000s perhaps lulled some into thinking that the lopsided design of Emu—a single currency without a single economic governance structure—was not a problem, but the double blows of the financial crisis from 2007 and the sovereign-debt crisis a couple of years later were certain to elevate them into matters of acute concern.

The roots of the financial crisis lay in the accelerated deregulation of financial markets in the early 2000s and the increasing lack of clarity about the structure of debts and obligations in the global system. The sudden collapse of many key market actors in 2007, as the scale and extent of exposure to bad debt became clear, resulted in a worldwide seizing up of credit. This in turn made banks unwilling or unable to make loans to businesses, forcing governments to turn to massive intervention via quantitative easing to return liquidity to markets.

In itself, this would have been manageable within Emu as it existed, since macroeconomic policy and bank regulation were still in national hands. However, from 2009 financial markets turned their attention away from banks to governments and, more particularly, their debts. In particular, markets became increasingly concerned that member states of the Eurozone were holding excessive amounts of sovereign (i.e. government) debt, to the extent that it potentially compromised their ability either to service that debt or to maintain the solvency of national banking systems, especially with national currency devaluation no longer being an option.

Eurozone membership certainly played a key role in this, as states that had previously had weaker fiscal management were able to benefit from the perceived extension of German rectitude across the Eurozone when issuing new debt, which could be sold at much lower rates than before. This encouraged a relaxing of fiscal management by those states compared to their earlier efforts to meet the entry requirements to the single currency; the Stability and Growth Pact (SGP) that had been introduced in the Amsterdam Treaty was a belated attempt to maintain the stricter regime. However, its regular flouting in the mid-2000s by most member states (including Germany and France) meant that it was a dead letter and that it was only the generally favourable macroeconomic climate that made it possible to sustain the situation.

From 2010 onwards, Eurozone leaders engaged in a series of emergency measures to try and regain the initiative. This included the creation in May 2010 of the European Financial Stability Facility (EFSF), with access to some €750 billion to provide extension support to Eurozone members. The EFSF has been the vehicle for the bailouts provided in support of three member states' situations to date, most notably Greece. These bailouts have been accompanied by requirements to implement significant supply-side reforms—including deregulation of working practices and the reduction of state ownership of many assets—in order to promote conditions for more sustainable long-term growth. The increased willingness of the ECB, under its President Mario Draghi, to provide cheap loans to banks and a backstop to sovereign debt since 2012 under the 'quantitative easing' programme has also acted as a means of relieving pressure, albeit temporarily.

If the EFSF and ECB have provided a short-term source of relief, then there has also been an effort to put in place long-term mechanisms in order to ensure that the crisis cannot occur again. This progressed in three main stages. Firstly, there was a reform of the SGP with the so-called 'Six-pack' of legislation passed in 2011 to allow for stricter enforcement of the SGP's provisions on excessive deficits: coupled to the Euro-Plus Pact and its supply-side reforms of Eurozone economies, this set out a framework for action. However, the limitations of this approach helped to push the EU and Eurozone into a second phase, from late 2011, when the European Fiscal Compact was agreed.

The compact, or the Treaty on Stability, Coordination and Governance in the Economic and Monetary Union (TSCG) as it is formally known, lies outside of the EU's legal framework, but can use the EU's institutions. This curious arrangement resulted from the unwillingness of the British government at the December 2011 European Council to agree to a treaty revision in the more usual fashion. This meant taking a more intergovernmental route to the compact's main objective of legal requirements for national budgets to be in balance. The compact provides for stronger monitoring and enforcement mechanisms at the European level, including the possibility of legal action before the Court of Justice. In so doing, the Eurozone has sought to give markets increased confidence in the long-term sustainability of the currency area.

In support of the compact, there was also agreement to move the EFSF onto a more permanent footing, with the creation in 2012 of the European Stability Mechanism (ESM). The ESM replaces the EFSF and provides a much more extensive set of financial reserves to support struggling Eurozone economies. In contrast to the compact, it sits firmly within the EU's system of enhanced cooperation, applying to all Eurozone members.

However, even with all this activity there was renewed pressure on the Eurozone, which in turn forced governments and the Commission back to the drawing board. This has led to several years of discussion about stronger economic governance, albeit with only limited progress. The most consequential element has been the creation of a banking union, which provides an integrated set of supervision and bailout mechanisms. Nonetheless, the consequence of all of these developments has been to move Emu into a new phase of its existence, where the pressures of very negative market forces have exposed the limitations of the asymmetric design laid out in the Maastricht Treaty. In so doing, Eurozone members have been forced to reinforce their commitment to the euro, and strengthen a number of key aspects of their economic and fiscal integration.

However, Emu does not lead inevitably to a federal state. A federal state extends its central powers over the use of force; and this does not follow from the adoption of the euro. The argument about defence integration, which is addressed later, is a different one. As regards strengthening the institutions and making them more democratic, that is already desirable, with or without the single currency; and it will become essential if the EU is to be capable of satisfying its citizens' needs and avoid the risk of disintegration.

Chapter 5

Agriculture, regions, budget: conflicts over who gets what

The single market is a positive-sum game—because it enhances productivity in the economy, there is benefit for most people, whether they take it in the form of consuming more or working less. But alongside the majority who gain, there will be some who lose, or at least fear they will lose, from the opening of markets to new competition; and these may demand compensation for agreeing to participate in the new arrangements. Such compensation usually has implications for the EU budget and looks like a zero-sum game, which can lead to conflict between those who pay and those who receive, even if the package of compensation and competition, taken together, benefits both parties. The first major example was the inclusion of agriculture in the EEC's common market.

Agriculture

The opening of the Community's market to trade in manufactures was, when the EEC was founded, a relatively simple matter of eliminating tariffs and quotas by stages. But tariff and quota disarmament was only a small part of the problem in creating an agricultural common market. All European countries managed their agricultural markets with complex devices such as subsidies and price supports to ensure adequate incomes for farmers and security of food supplies. So a common market for agriculture would have to be a complicated managed market for the EEC, to replace those of the member states. It would have been simpler to confine the common market to industry. But the French feared the prospect of German industrial competition and, themselves having a competitive agricultural sector, they insisted that the EEC market be opened to agriculture too.

The result was the common agricultural policy, with prices of the main products supported at levels decided by the Council of Ministers, through variable levies on imports from outside the Community and purchase of surplus production into storage at the support level. Farmers' incomes were bolstered by high prices paid by the consumer, together with subsidies from the Community's taxpayers to finance the surpluses that resulted from the high prices. While this was tenable in the EEC's early years, once the UK became a member new tensions arose. The British model of free trade had meant that prices had been much lower, so membership of the CAP meant a triple blow of: higher prices for food; high levels of British contributions to the budget because of import levies on foodstuffs; and low receipts from the budget because of the small size of its agricultural sector.

This state of affairs was to trigger a five-year battle after Mrs Thatcher became Prime Minister in 1979, as she blocked much other EC business in her bid to '[get] our money back'. Matters came to a head in 1984, when the accumulation of stocks such as 'butter mountains' and 'wine lakes' had cost so much that the EEC needed to raise the ceiling for its revenue from taxation; and this required unanimous agreement by the member states. So a deal was done, including an annual rebate for Britain at around two-thirds of its net contribution. At the same time steps were taken to reform the CAP, but only modest steps, because attention was focused on questions of rebate and tax resources.

Stages of reform

The CAP lumbered on, accumulating further costly surpluses, until 1988 when the money ran out again. This time the financial interests of member states prevailed. With the division of the Council of Ministers into functional formations, the decisions of the agriculture ministers on prices of farm products had determined the level of the bulk of EC expenditure, over which finance ministers in Ecofin had little say. Since the resulting bill had to be paid out of EC tax resources, the agriculture ministers were in effect deciding on the rate of EC tax paid by all EC member states' citizens. Financial control had to be established and the European Council agreed in 1988 on a package of measures, proposed by Delors, which introduced a 'financial perspective' setting limits for the main areas of EC expenditure during the five years, 1988–92. Any increase in spending on agriculture was restricted to less than three-quarters of the rate of growth of total EC spending.

While this took some of the heat out of the conflict over money, a serious reform of the CAP was still required. By 1992 the Commissioner responsible for agriculture was Ray MacSharry, a former Irish minister. He grasped the nettle and, outmanoeuvring the opposition, secured a cut of 15 per cent in the support price for beef and nearly one-third for cereals. The existing levels of expenditure were not reduced, because farmers were compensated with income supports, including 'set-aside' payments for leaving cultivated land to lie fallow. But the measures quashed the expansionary dynamic from the CAP and prepared the ground for further reform.

The cost of the CAP remained a heavy burden for the EU, with half the budget going to support a sector that employs less than 5 per cent of the working population, much of it for a small minority of the bigger and richer farmers (see Chart 3). By the

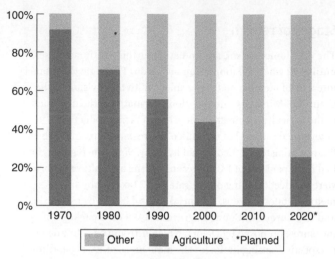

Chart 3. Share of budget spent on agriculture, 1970–2020.

end of the 1990s, moreover, the twin pressures of enlargement to the east and negotiations within the newly established World Trade Organization (WTO) were forcing the EU into a greater focus on structural reform. New member states, with their large agricultural sectors, were set to drive up costs very significantly, while the need to secure agreement in WTO trade liberalization negotiations was placing increasing pressure on reductions in levels of agricultural support. Consequently, the EU agreed substantial cuts for some products in 1999, as part of wider budgetary negotiations, as well as introducing the notion of a multifunctional CAP (i.e. one that extends into the social and environmental dimensions that surround farming). This recasting of the CAP as a 'rural' policy—confirmed by the 2008 'health check'—was an important step in helping to unblock the reforms that some states, notably France, had put on hold.

This became much more apparent at the mid-term review of the 1999 agreement in 2003, with what had initially been considered a simple review of the changes producing reforms as important as those of MacSharry a decade previously. Again the level of price support was cut, but the main revolution was the shift towards direct support for farmers. Until then, the CAP had used price support mechanisms to pay farmers, thus providing a strong incentive to overproduce: hence the wine lakes and butter mountains of the 1980s. The new Single Farm Payment (SFP) introduced in 2006 separates (or 'decouples', in the jargon) payment from production: instead farmers are paid to look after their land, regardless of whether they choose to farm it or not.

The breaking of the old model of price support was perhaps inevitable in the face of the pressures that the CAP had faced over the previous forty years. The combination of enlargement, WTO negotiations, rising environmental concerns, and public health scares ultimately proved too powerful to resist. Despite new member states supporting a CAP that makes substantial payments to farmers, the notion of a more multifunctional approach to rural development has become a much more dominant discourse within the institutions and is likely to lead to yet more change.

Cohesion and structural funds

The 'cohesion policy', the other big item of expenditure in the EU's budget, has been a happier experience than the CAP. It stems from fears in member states with weaker economies that they would lose out in free competition within the EU. When the customs union, the single market, and the single currency were established, funds were provided to assist their economic development so that they could cooperate in these new ventures and become prosperous partners—hence the word 'cohesion'.

The first such provision was for the Social Fund, included at Italy's request in the Treaty of Rome. Italy's economy was the weakest of the six founding states, and Italians feared they would suffer from the liberalization of trade. They wanted a fund to help their workforce to adapt; and their demand was met, though on quite a small scale.

The motive for establishing the European Regional Development Fund (ERDF) was somewhat different. By the time of British accession in 1973, Britain's economic performance had fallen behind those of the six founder states; and there was the prospect of the big net contribution for the CAP. Britain had its share and more of regions with economic difficulties, but other member states had theirs too. Edward Heath's government, which had negotiated British accession, had the sound idea that a fund for regional assistance would both respond to a general interest and be of particular value to Britain, not only assisting its regional development but also reducing its net contribution to the Community budget. While the initial impact of the fund was weak, it has developed into the main source of financing for cohesion.

The third of what became known as the 'structural funds', in order to underline that their aim was not just to redistribute money but rather to improve economic performance in the weaker parts of the EU's economy, is the European Agricultural Fund for Rural Development (formerly the 'Guidance Section' of the European Agricultural Guarantee and Guidance Fund (EAGGF)), which helps farmers carry out structural change. But the three structural funds, though at first small, grew steadily and were available to respond to the demand for a major expansion in the 1980s when the EC expanded to the south.

Enlargement and structural funds

When Spain, Portugal, and Greece joined the EC, their average incomes were far below those of the other member states save Ireland, which before its phenomenal growth in the 1990s was at a similar level. These four countries, led by Spain, demanded a major increase in the structural funds and their ability to block agreement on the passage of the single market legislation meant the Single Act contained an article on 'economic and social cohesion'; Delors proposed that the budget for the structural funds be doubled in the financial perspective for 1988–92; and this was accepted by the European Council.

A similar problem emerged when it was decided to embark on Emu, with the same four states seeking a similar expansion of the structural funds. This time Delors secured an increase of two-fifths in the allocation for the period 1993–9; and the Maastricht Treaty provided for the establishment of the Cohesion Fund, to support projects in the fields of the environment and transport infrastructure. By 2000 the budget for the funds was €32 billion (see Box 2).

Box 2 Structural funds and objectives

Since the early 1970s, the Community has developed its regional policies around a set of funds and objectives. These were reformed in 1999 and again in 2006.

The Structural Funds now comprise:

- the ERDF—deals with regional development and economic change;
- the ESF—concerned with re-training workers;
- Cohesion Fund—aimed at poorer member states, this fund develops projects in the environment and infrastructure.

Since 2014, spending has been integrated across these funds to support eleven thematic objectives, covering improvements in competitiveness and research, environmental protection, infrastructure development, labour force support, and aid for modernizing public administration. In the period 2014–20, about €50 billion per year is due to be spent on projects in every member state.

The four states for which the expansion of the structural funds was originally designed have performed for the most part well, the current Eurozone crisis notwithstanding. Spain has been very successful, though less outstandingly so than Ireland; Portugal had to check its initially rapid growth with a stabilization programme. The Greek case has been much more complex, with the finance available through the funds being counteracted by more structural macroeconomic problems. While it is not possible to say how much of this generally good result can be attributed to the structural funds, the contributions of 2–4 per cent of GDP certainly eased the path.

Although the objectives of the structural funds had focused on help for regions where development was 'lagging behind', it has always been a feature of cohesion policy that all member states get something back out of the budget. Partly this is a reflection of the diversity of the states, but it is also driven by the unanimity required to conclude budgetary planning negotiations. This posed a particular problem with the enlargement to the east, since under the policy that prevailed in the late 1990s, new member states stood to receive very large amounts of funding, while existing member states stood to lose out.

The response to this was, as with the CAP, to engage in some fairly drastic reforms. The growth in funding for cohesion was capped in the financial perspective agreed at Berlin in 1999, since richer member states were not prepared to foot the bill, while simultaneously it was decided that most of the existing funding should be ring-fenced for existing members, regardless of new members' objective needs. Coupled with the Commission's pronouncement that transfers to any member state would be capped to the equivalent of 4 per cent of GDP, on the grounds that this was the most any country could usefully absorb, when enlargement did come in 2004 its impacts on the budget were relatively attenuated. Even as funding has continued to flow towards Central and Eastern Europe, the ability of individual

governments to translate that into sustainable economic and
social development has been mixed, as those states have found
that lack of money alone is not the sole issue. In the more recent
2014–20 funding cycle, this has been reflected in the increased
profile of support for mobilizing public administration and other
societal structures to encourage a stronger environment for
development to occur.

Thus while the cohesion policy has, unlike the CAP, been relatively
harmonious, it is important to recognize the limitations that member
states have placed on maximizing its benefit for the EU as a whole.
This posture has also increasingly affected the budget as a whole.

The budget

With agriculture and cohesion now accounting for about 40 per
cent each of EU expenditure, the two together, with their powerfully
redistributive effects, account for the bulk of spending. The cost
of administration of EU institutions comes to less than 6 per cent
of the total, and the remainder goes to finance a range of internal
and external policies (see Chart 4).

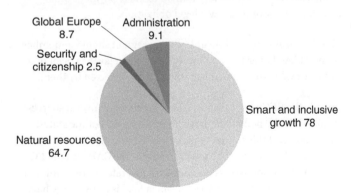

Total: €163.0 billion

Chart 4. Breakdown of budget expenditure, 2015 (€ billion).

The total expenditure in the budget for 2017 was €157.9 billion, or 1.04 per cent of EU GNP. This has to remain below 1.23 per cent of GNP unless that ceiling is raised by a decision ratified by all the member states; and the financial perspective for the years 2014–20 keeps spending below 1.23 per cent of GNP in each year.

'Own resources'

Unlike international organizations that depend on contributions from their member states, the EU's revenue from taxes is a legal requirement under the treaty, subject, like other treaty obligations, to the authority of the Court of Justice. This is to prevent member states from holding the EU to ransom by withholding contributions. The consequences of such behaviour are demonstrated by the financial state of the United Nations (UN), weakened for many years by the refusal of Congress to sanction payment of the US contribution—ironically enough, since the failure of American states to pay their contributions in the 1780s under the Articles of Confederation was a powerful argument in favour of the establishment of the US federal constitution. The same argument influenced the EC's founding fathers to make payment of tax revenue to the Community a legal obligation.

The EU has no physical means of enforcement should a member state not hand over the money. But the rule of law has been of sufficient value to the member states to be respected by them.

Initially the EEC's tax revenue, called in the treaty 'own resources' to underline the point that they belong to the EC not the states, comprised the takings from customs duties and agricultural import levies. But these were not enough to pay for the CAP, and the EC was allocated a share of value-added tax at a rate of 1 per cent of the value of the goods and services on which VAT is levied (see Chart 5).

A major objection to these indirect taxes was that they hit the poorer states and citizens hard, making them pay a higher

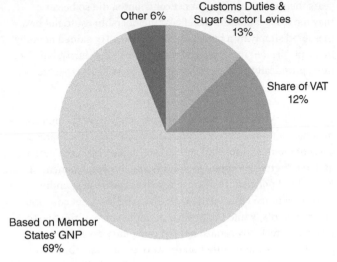

Other 6%

Customs Duties &
Sugar Sector Levies
13%

Share of VAT
12%

Based on Member
States' GNP
69%

Chart 5. Sources of revenue, 2015.

proportion of incomes than those who are richer. So in 1988 a fourth resource was introduced, in the form of a small percentage of the GNP of each member state. This is roughly proportional to incomes and now accounts for almost three-quarters of the EU's revenue. But the total outcome of the revenue system is still regressive.

Net contributions

As already mentioned, it was Mrs Thatcher who first coined the phrase '[getting] our money back', although the British had, since their accession in 1973, been constantly seeking redress for what they could claim to be an 'unacceptable situation' resulting from a financial regulation adopted just before they joined. Previously, the fact that some member states got more out of the budget than others was taken simply as part of the package of membership. In particular, the Germans, who had willingly accepted for many years their role as the largest net contributor, did so because they recognized that the benefits of membership could not be measured simply by a bank balance: the country gained not only in deeply desired international acceptance and security, but also, more prosaically, in giving German exporters access to large new markets.

None the less, since the 1980s, and particularly since the mid-1990s, member states have become much more aware of the financial costs of membership. This was driven in part by Mrs Thatcher and her energetic campaign, but also by the development of EC and EU policies. The large growth of cohesion spending further reinforced the north–south divide between net contributors and recipients, while the growth in importance of the fourth resource effectively renationalized budgetary receipts. In addition, existing member states were concerned about the budgetary implications of enlargement. Coupled to Germany's increasing reluctance to foot the bills, reform became increasingly inevitable.

In 1999, the Berlin European Council agreed to reduce the amount that Germany, the Netherlands, Austria, and Sweden, the then net contributors, paid towards the British rebate. That rebate remained a bone of contention, since the original case of over-contributions and under-receipts was less and less compelling, but successive British governments were loath to give up an income stream of several billion pounds a year. None the less, as enlargement became a reality, the British did demonstrate some willingness to reduce the level of their rebate in order to minimize the burden on the new member states, agreeing in 2005 to take a reduction of the rebate of €10.5 billion between 2007 and 2013, equivalent to roughly one-quarter of the total value. This was intended to help the British case for a more general review of spending policies and budgetary procedure, although the current 2014–20 financial perspectives show little sign of this.

Box 3 States' net budgetary payments or receipts

Net contributors		Net recipients	
Belgium	−0.43	Cyprus	0.04
Netherlands	−0.36	Ireland	0.04
Denmark	−0.36	Spain	0.17
Luxembourg	−0.35	Malta	0.21
Germany	−0.33	Slovenia	0.75
Italy	−0.27	Slovakia	0.93
France	−0.25	Czech Republic	1.34
Finland	−0.25	Portugal	1.39
Sweden	−0.24	Greece	1.44
Austria	−0.16	Romania	1.51
United Kingdom	−0.09	Bulgaria	1.88
		Poland	2.16
		Latvia	2.58
		Hungary	3.17
		Estonia	4.37
Croatia	n/a	Lithuania	5.57

Source: European Commission, *EU Budget 2015 Financial Report*, 2016.
Note: percentage of GNI, 2015; − = net payments.

Of more concern is the lack of growth in the EU's budget overall. Since 1999, there has been a reduction in the ceiling of expenditure as a percentage of GNP (see Box 3). Even with the growth of that GNP over time, the budget remains very small in comparison with member state governments' budgets. This is a somewhat unfair comparison, since the EU does not have to spend on social security, defence, health, education, or any of the major items that we typically associate with public activities. However, the size of the budget does constrain what the EU can do, for example in promoting cohesion and balanced development across all its member states. While it does appear to have weathered the transition to an enlarged membership, it is evident that further reforms will be needed if the EU is to remain a relevant actor, both internally and in the wider world.

Chapter 6
Social policy, environmental policy

The EU has been given some of its powers, such as those to establish the single market, because its size offers advantages that are beyond the reach of the individual member states. Other powers are designed to prevent member states from damaging each other. The environment is one field in which powers have been given to that end, with general agreement that it is desirable. Another is social policy, where there has been sharp disagreement as to how far EU intervention is required.

Social policy

The term 'social policy' has a narrower meaning in EU parlance than it generally has in Britain. It does not refer to the range of policies, including health, housing, and social services, with which the welfare state is concerned. The pattern of such services differs from country to country, reflecting their political and social cultures; and it is widely accepted that the cross-border effects of the differences are not sufficient to justify intervention by the EU. In treaty and EU jargon, however, social policy concerns matters relating to employment, where there are also wide variations from country to country. But since conditions of employment touch more closely on the single market, there has been pressure to harmonize member states' policies in order to prevent employees in states with higher standards suffering as a result of competition from those with lower standards.

The first such example was the article on equal pay in the Treaty of Rome. France was ahead of other founder states in having legislated that women be paid equally with men for equal work. In order to keep sectors that employed a high proportion of women competitive, France demanded that its partners introduce equal pay too. With the general movement towards gender equality, this was to become one of the most popular European laws. By the time of the Amsterdam Treaty, there was ready agreement to extend the principle from equal pay to equal opportunities and equal treatment in all matters relating to employment.

The Single European Act extended the scope of social policy in two directions: providing for legislation on health and safety at work and for the encouragement of dialogue between representatives of management and labour at a European level. While Mrs Thatcher had fought hard against the influence of 'corporatist' relationships in Britain, she doubtless reckoned that such dialogue at a European level would not be of much consequence; and the case against undercutting standards of health and safety was generally agreed. So although EC social policy was to become one of Thatcher's bêtes noires, she accepted these provisions of the Single Act as part of the package that included the single market programme.

In 1989, Delors, who saw higher standards of social legislation as being, for workers, a necessary counterpart to the single market, proposed a social charter that was approved by all but one in the European Council. Thatcher dissented. Although she accepted some of its provisions, such as free movement for workers and the right to join (or not) a trade union, she contested others, such as the right for workers to participate in companies' decision-taking, as well as a maximum number of working hours—which, much to the British government's disgust, were subsequently enacted by a qualified majority vote under the treaty article on health and safety at work. Major followed her example when he secured Britain's opt-out from the provisions on social policy in the Maastricht Treaty, which therefore appeared in a protocol that applied to all the other member states. It was only after Labour's election victory in 1997 that there was unanimous agreement to convert the protocol into a social chapter in the Amsterdam Treaty; and it was accompanied by a new chapter aimed at achieving 'a high level of employment and of social protection'. But Britain has continued to promote the cause of flexible labour markets, an objective that was taken up in the 2000 Lisbon Agenda and its successor the 2010 'Europe 2020', which brought together social policy with employment policy in a combination that was much more oriented to the use of economic growth to provide for social well-being.

The relative success of British and Irish economic performance since the 1990s has helped to give credibility to a more Anglo-Saxon approach in social matters—based on deregulation and flexibility, rather than interventionist policies (see Box 4). But more important still has been the sustained success of the American economy, with its low unemployment and high growth, from which the conclusion could be drawn that flexibility suits the current stage of technological development. While the degree of laissez-faire in the American approach to social policy is resisted, a certain consensus may be emerging in the EU that methods such as bench-marking and peer pressure are more suitable than social legislation for reducing unemployment, as well as for some measures to create a dynamic and competitive economy. While there is still a strong constituency within several large member states for an interventionist approach to such questions, the rise of globalization, the need to maintain competitiveness, and the Eurozone crisis have moved the debate within the EU towards the British viewpoint over time, albeit with limited legislation at the European level.

Box 4 Employment policy

The Amsterdam Treaty introduced a new section on employment in response to concern about the high level of unemployment in the EU. Its main purpose was to encourage cooperation among the member states with respect to their employment policies.

The member states provide annual reports on their employment policies to the Council of Ministers and Commission, which draw up a report for the European Council, working with the headline targets of the Europe 2020 Strategy on jobs and growth. Guidelines are then issued to the states to be taken into account in their employment policies; and the Council of Ministers can make recommendations to governments. The Council of Ministers, in co-decision with the Parliament, may decide to spend money from the budget to encourage exchanges of information and best practices, provide comparative analysis and advice, promote innovative approaches, and fund pilot projects.

The impact on governments' policies has remained limited, as member states continue to be driven by national political imperatives.

Environmental policy

Polluted air and water cannot be prevented from moving out of one state and causing damage in another. So there is an interest in common standards to control the pollution at its source. The same applies to the environmental effects of goods traded in the single market. The Single European Act provided for an EC environmental policy to deal with these problems. It also affirmed that the EC's objective was to 'preserve, protect and improve the quality of the environment'.

Several hundred environmental measures have been enacted, responding to a wide range of environmental concerns: air and water pollution; waste disposal; noise limits for aircraft and motor vehicles; wildlife habitats; quality standards for drinking and bathing water. In 1988 a law was passed to reduce the incidence of acid rain, cutting emissions of sulphur dioxide and nitrogen oxides by 58 per cent by stages over the subsequent fifteen years. Standards of protection against dangerous chemicals were demanded following the accession of the environmentally conscious Swedes in 1995; and the highly complex REACH regulation for guaranteeing standards throughout the EU was finally passed in 2006. While EU legislation had always allowed member states to set their own higher standards in other matters, Scandinavian pressure led to an article in the Amsterdam Treaty allowing states to have higher standards for traded products too, provided they can persuade the Commission that these are not protectionist devices; and by 2004, the 'polluter pays' principle became EU law. The focus on environmental policy came at a time when Europeans were rapidly becoming greener, so it became one of the EU's most popular policies, as the provision for equal pay had been before; and, like policy for gender equality, it too was strengthened by the Amsterdam Treaty, which stipulated that 'environmental protection requirements' must be integrated into other EU policies 'with a view to promoting sustainable development'.

The Sixth Environmental Action Programme, which the Council of Ministers and Parliament approved in 2002, contained a ten-year framework for promoting sustainable development, in the fields of climate change, nature and biodiversity, environment and health, and natural resources and waste. Later in that year the EU played a leading role in the World Summit on Sustainable Development in South Africa. Sustainable development strategy has subsequently been a priority, with climate change being the most prominent element, gaining an explicit mention in the Lisbon Treaty.

The EU's action with respect to climate change has had a powerful impact, both internally and in the wider world. The EU signed the Kyoto Protocol in 1998, with its target of cutting emissions of greenhouse gases by 2012 to 8 per cent below the 1990 level. The Council of Ministers then, in a somewhat fraught process, allocated quotas to the member states for their emissions, on a proposal from the Commission after consultation with each state, to a total estimated to keep the EU's emissions within the target. The emissions are carefully monitored and there are penalties for non-compliance. In 2005 the EU, in order to provide flexibility in the control of emissions, introduced its Emissions Trading Scheme (ETS), which allocates the rights among more than 5,000 of the EU's major industrial polluters, allowing those that emit less than their quotas to sell the unused rights to those that use more, and thus creating a 'carbon market' which determines the cost of carbon within the EU. Since the rights were evidently issued too generously initially, the ETS will now auction credits, helping to raise the carbon price to a high enough level to discourage excessive use. This is particularly important since the European Council decided in 2006, following the best scientific advice, that the EU must achieve a 60 per cent cut by 2050, in line with the global target deemed necessary to avoid potentially catastrophic change; and since, as is shown in Chapter 10, the EU is leading the world in this field, it needs to maintain its own credibility.

Chapter 7
'An area of freedom, security and justice'

Ernest Bevin, the great Foreign Secretary in the first post-war Labour government, said that the aim of his foreign policy 'really was...to grapple with the whole problem of passports and visas', so that he could 'go down to Victoria Station', where trains departed for the Continent, 'get a railway ticket, and go where the Hell I liked without a passport or anything else'. The old trade unionist retained his vision of the brotherhood of man. But the Foreign Minister found himself defending the sovereignty of states; and he rejected the idea of British membership of the emergent Community, which was eventually to make the realization of his vision feasible in Europe.

Already in 1958 the Rome Treaty included 'persons', along with goods, services, and capital, in the four freedoms of movement across the frontiers between the member states. For 'persons' this was limited to the right to cross frontiers for purposes of work. A quarter of a century later, the Single European Act defined the internal market as 'an area without internal frontiers'. Mrs Thatcher's government held that these words implied no change, because they were qualified by the addition 'in accordance with the Treaty', which in relevant respects still stood. But governments of the more federalist states intended to take the words literally: to abolish controls at their mutual borders and thus make movement across them free for all.

This idea was given legal expression in the Schengen Agreements of 1985 and 1990, Schengen being the small town in Luxembourg, symbolically alongside the frontiers with both France and Germany, where these three states, together with Belgium and the Netherlands, signed the agreements. The number of signatories has since grown until what has often been called Schengenland has been signed up to by most EU states, as well as by European Free Trade Association (Efta) members: only Britain and Ireland have opt-outs.

Schengen had two main aims. The first concerned border controls: to eliminate those internal to Schengenland; establish controls round its external frontier; and set rules to deal with asylum, immigration, and the movement or residence of other countries' nationals within the area. The second was to cooperate in combating crime.

Cross-border criminal activity grows for reasons similar to those that drive cross-border economic activity: advancing technology, particularly in transport and communications. As with trade, cross-border cooperation is needed if the rule of law is to keep abreast of it. With the intense relationship engendered by their economic integration, the member states have a special need for such cooperation. A first step was taken in 1974 with the 'Trevi' agreement to exchange information about terrorism; and the ministers and officials involved soon found it useful to include other forms of crime. This was a precursor of Schengen, which forged closer cooperation among law enforcement agencies of the states that were ready to go further together, and which has led to an extensive 'acquis' of legal texts, applying to the very large majority of EU member states.

Maastricht's third pillar

Cross-border aspects of crime and the movement of people affect all member states, not just those of Schengenland. It was agreed that the Maastricht Treaty should provide for cooperation in these fields. Terrorism, drugs, fraud, and 'other serious forms of crime' were listed in the treaty, along with external border controls, asylum, immigration, and movement across the internal borders by nationals from states outside the EU. The member states' judicial, administrative, police, and customs authorities were to cooperate in order to deal with them.

Some states, such as Germany, wanted this to be done within the EC institutions, with the Commission, Court of Justice, and Parliament as well as the Council of Ministers playing their normal parts. Others, such as Britain, defending their sovereignty, wanted to exclude as far as possible any institutions other than the Council of Ministers. The upshot was that the new 'third pillar' for Cooperation in Justice and Home Affairs (CJHA) was set up alongside the EC 'first pillar'. The institutions for the CJHA were intergovernmental, with the unanimity procedure in the Council of Ministers, only consultative roles for the Parliament and Commission, and very limited jurisdiction for the Court of Justice. The policy instruments were to be joint positions and actions determined by the Council of Ministers, and conventions ratified by all the member states. One of the conventions was to establish the new policing body, Europol.

Not surprisingly, given the requirement of unanimous agreement among the then fifteen governments before a decision could be taken, there had not been much progress by the time the Amsterdam Treaty was negotiated. No convention had yet entered into force and action in other respects was slow. But concern about cross-border crime and illegal immigration continued to grow; and Eastern European enlargement, expected to bring new problems, was approaching. So most member states wanted a stronger system.

Amsterdam's project

The Amsterdam Treaty affirmed the intention to establish what it rather grandly called 'an area of freedom, security and justice'

(AFSJ). This essentially meant that various third pillar elements moved into the first pillar, under the EU's institutional control, most notably by Parliament and the Court of Justice. Coupled to a new cycle of five-yearly programmes from 1999, and with the gradual adoption of the Charter of Fundamental Rights, AFSJ developed considerable momentum.

Lisbon brought further substantive change. The collapsing of the pillars has brought police and judicial cooperation into the Ordinary Legislative Procedure, albeit with member states being allowed a limited right of initiative. While the Charter is now legally binding, several states, including the UK, have special provisions, reflecting the continued sensitivity of the policy field.

While conditions in the EU are, in a general sense, notably free, secure, and just when compared with almost all other parts of the world, the words are used in the treaty in a more specific sense: 'freedom' refers to free movement across internal borders; 'security', to protection against cross-border crime; and 'justice', mainly to judicial cooperation in civil as well as criminal matters.

As regards *freedom* of movement, almost all the Schengen acquis has already been transferred into the EU. Thus the right of people to move freely throughout Schengenland is guaranteed by the institutions, though some member states have had to restore border checks temporarily in order to deal with influxes from other member states of non-EU nationals with false visas. The external border controls are not yet satisfactory. Nor is the common policy on immigration and asylum complete. Nor will there be freedom of movement without border checks throughout the EU while Britain, Denmark, and Ireland retain their controls. Brexit might resolve the British exception, and possibly the Irish one too, although this will depend on the post-membership arrangements for free movement on the island of Ireland. However, the Danish referendum in 2015 that confirmed its opt-out status makes it very unlikely that this will change, especially given the (increasingly protracted) 'temporary' suspensions of Schengen provisions by various states in the wake of the refugee crisis since 2016.

As regards *security*, the fight against cross-border crime remains primarily intergovernmental, albeit with extending influence of the Commission. There has been significant activity addressing trafficking in persons, offences against children, corruption, money-laundering, forging money, and 'cyber-crime'. Europol has made a useful contribution, though it could not become fully operational until its convention was fully ratified by all member states in July 1999, over five years after the Maastricht Treaty had provided for it. Likewise, Frontex, established in 2005 to coordinate border guards, now deploys teams to several of the EU's key frontiers, most notably in the Mediterranean.

However, it is in the field of counter-terrorism that most significant progress has been made. After the September 2001 attacks on the US, the EU quickly pushed to develop its own abilities to act. A European arrest warrant that had been in limbo for several years was agreed in 2002, alongside an action plan that targets aspects of the prevention and prosecution of terrorist acts, as well as coordinating responses by member states. Linked to this was the decision to create a high-level European police college and a body called Eurojust, bringing together member states' prosecutors, magistrates, and police officers to cooperate in criminal investigation and prosecution.

In the narrow definition of *justice* as judicial cooperation, some specific steps have been taken for member states to assist each other in cross-border problems relating to the recognition and enforcement of judgments, though not much has been done about the rights of victims of crime. The path chosen by the EU has been one of mutual recognition, rather than harmonization; but there has been agreement on several joint policies, most notably the European arrest warrant, which address some of the problems of cross-border crime.

In a broader definition of the word, distributive justice has been an issue in this field since Germany, with a much larger number of asylum-seekers than other member states, wanted measures to share the cost. This resulted in the creation of a European asylum policy that has coordinated national policies, albeit with limits so painfully exposed by the 2015 migrant crisis.

In a yet broader sense of justice, the EU has responded to criticism that it emphasized restrictions on immigration and asylum at the expense of concern about the treatment of the human beings involved. In the face of a widespread public backlash against them, the Amsterdam Treaty provided for measures to safeguard their rights, together with action more generally to combat racism and xenophobia. Coupled to the Charter on Fundamental Rights, the EU has now articulated a fairly substantial human rights protection programme, although the degree to which it can enforce this remains moot.

What's in the name?

Freedom of movement within Schengenland is an almost complete reality, recent suspensions notwithstanding. If Bevin were able to go to the Gare du Nord or the Gare de Lyon today, he could buy a ticket and go without a passport wherever he liked within Schengenland, though not, unfortunately, to Victoria Station.

While Lisbon has brought much clarity to the organization of this policy field, it is far from certain this goes far enough to tackle the various challenges. The persisting divisions between member states and the EU, as well as the differential memberships of the

EU and Schengenland, result in confused lines of control, limited scope for action, and a system that few members of the public either know or understand. In many ways, the Area of Freedom, Security and Justice is a classic example of the EU's wider problem: it is a potentially useful means for tackling problems that are beyond the scope of individual member states, but it is hampered by the political compromises, abstruse jargon, and occasionally counter-intuitive policies that result from trying to bring together such a large number of actors without adequate institutional reform.

Chapter 8
A great civilian power...and more—or less?

The main motives for creating the EC were peace between France, Germany, and the other member states, and prosperity for their citizens. But while their mutual relationship was a particular focus of attention, relations with their neighbours and countries further afield were also very important; and the logic of subsidiarity (i.e. that the Community should have responsibility for doing what it is better able to do than its member states acting separately) began to be applied to external as well as internal affairs.

The EC's external relations were, in line with its powers, originally concentrated in the economic field. But there were from the outset also political aims. For Germany, bordering on the Soviet bloc, and with East Germany under Soviet control, the priority was solidarity in resistance to Soviet pressure. The French had a broader vision of the EC as a power in the world. Relations with the US were a central element: for Monnet, in the form of a partnership between the EC and the US; and for de Gaulle, to defy American hegemony. Monnet's view was widely shared and the EC came to be seen as a potential 'great civilian power'.

Many in France went beyond this, envisaging a Europe that could challenge American dominance in the field of defence. In other countries this view was generally resisted. But cooperation in foreign policy evolved to the point where the EU gave it the name

'Common Foreign and Security Policy'; and Britain, which had long been adamantly opposed to common action by the EU on defence, in 1999 joined France in initiating a modest EU defence capacity. This is still a minor, though increasingly significant, element in the EU's external relations. The EU's external economic policies remain much more important.

Meanwhile, the world has been becoming a more dangerous place, with sources of instability such as climate change, environmental degradation, cross-border crime, poverty, consequent mass migration, and terrorism, alongside military forms of insecurity. The relative simplicity of the confrontation between the US and the Soviet Union has been replaced by American supremacy, and with the perspective of an emergent multipolar world in which the US is in the process of being joined by China and, probably later, India as giant powers, while Russia along with other, rising powers must also be taken into account; and the balance of bipolar economic power, with the predominance of the US and the EU, is being rapidly transformed, likewise with the BRIC economies of China, India, Russia, and Brazil, into a multipolar world economy. This is the world in which the EU has to find its place.

Europeans have generally reached a stage in their history, and particularly in the experience of living peaceably together in the EU, when they greatly value security and predictability in their relations between member states, and hence they favour the creation of a secure multilateral system worldwide. While the EU's military capabilities play a growing part in functions such as peacekeeping, its external economic, aid, and environmental policies, together with its experience in developing peaceful relations among states, have a major potential for contributing to both its own security and prosperity, and that of those in the wider world. In this perspective, much can be learned from the EU's experience so far. So we examine in this chapter why and how its structures for dealing with the rest of the world have been established; in

Chapter 9, how it has come to be enlarged from fifteen states in Western Europe to include most other European states; and, in Chapter 10, how its policies for dealing with the rest of the world have been developed.

External economic relations

The Rome Treaty gave the EEC its common external tariff as an instrument for trade policy, called in the jargon 'common commercial policy'. This was not a foregone conclusion. Some wanted the member states to keep their existing tariffs: below the average in Germany and Benelux; higher in France and Italy. But the French insisted on the common tariff, partly because they feared competition from cheap imports seeping through the low-tariff states, but partly also because they wanted the EC to have an instrument with which it could start to become a force in world affairs (see Chart 6).

This has remained a persistent French theme. It was one of the motives for the drive towards the single currency, challenging the hegemony of the dollar; and it has continued with the effort to build a European defence capacity, for which the term 'Europe puissance' has been coined, contrasted with a mere European 'space' preoccupied with business affairs. Neither those French who were highly protectionist nor the British who at that time criticized the common tariff as a protectionist device envisaged that it would in fact be the trigger for the Kennedy Round of tariff cuts, which was the first step towards the EC's role as the foremost promoter of world trade liberalization, and thus also towards demonstrating the power of a common instrument of external policy.

That power has been seen in the field of agriculture too, with much less fortunate results. The system of import levies and export subsidies has been used in a highly protectionist way, to the detriment of the EC's consumers and international trade

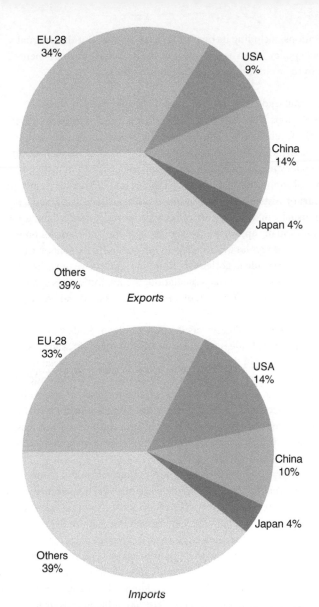

Chart 6. Shares of world merchandise trade of the EU, the US, China, Japan, and others, 2015.

relations, including its own industrial exports. But the external trade policy, taken as a whole, has been of considerable benefit both to its citizens and to international trade.

External trade relations are conducted effectively by the EU institutions. Policies are decided and trade agreements approved by the Council of Ministers under the procedure of qualified majority; negotiations are conducted by the Commission within the policy mandate thus decided, and in consultation with a special committee appointed by the Council of Ministers; and the Court of Justice has jurisdiction on points of law. Parliaments do not usually play much part in relation to trade negotiations, apart from formally approving the results. But while the treaties only provide for regular briefing of the European Parliament on the progress of trade negotiations, and the right to give or withhold its assent over treaties of association, the institution has come to play a significant part in external relations more generally.

When the Rome Treaty was drafted, trade in goods was all-important: trade in services was of little account, and was not mentioned in the chapter on the common commercial policy. But services now comprise about one-third of all world trade, so there has had to be a progressive extension of the EU system into most service areas. Qualified majority voting is now the norm in all services, save in the fields of culture, audio-visual services, education, health and social services, and some transport services.

Development aid has also become a major instrument of the EU's external policy, initiated, likewise on French insistence, with the Rome Treaty's provision for a fund for the then colonies of member states. This has since burgeoned so that the EU provides aid for countries throughout the less-developed parts of the world. Thus the EU, together with its member states, has become by far the world's largest source of aid; and within Europe the EU's instruments of trade and aid policy, along with the prospect of membership, have been a major external influence favouring the successful transformation of the new member states from Central and Eastern Europe. It was indeed fortunate that France insisted on the original grant of instruments for the Community's external policy.

The environment too, and climate change in particular, has become a major field for international negotiation; and though the EU's external policy remains subject to a somewhat more intergovernmental procedure than its trade policy, the EU has nonetheless, as we shall see in Chapter 10, had a decisive impact on negotiations to counter global warming and the destruction of the ozone layer.

The EU does not yet play a similar part in the international monetary system, despite the potential offered by the Eurozone crisis. The institutional arrangements for conducting an external monetary policy are not at present strong enough to enable it to exert its potential weight, although the ECB has clearly become an important player in policy debates.

Foreign policy

Cooperation in foreign policy among the member states was introduced in 1970 as an element of deepening as well as widening to include Britain, Ireland, and Denmark. The name given to this activity was European Political Cooperation (EPC): the word 'political' being used by ministries of foreign affairs, distinguishing what they saw as 'high politics' from such matters as economics, evidently regarded as low. But the EC's external economic policies were already a great deal more important than anything the EPC was to achieve during the following years, particularly as France, in the early years after de Gaulle, insisted that the EPC be kept not only intergovernmental but also rigorously separate from the EEC.

The EPC did achieve an important early result when the member states got human rights placed on the agenda of the Conference on Security and Cooperation in Europe. The Soviet Union accepted the text that was finally adopted, which, though nobody then thought it of much consequence, in the event gave support to the agitation that contributed to the dissolution of the Soviet bloc. More generally, the member states' diplomats developed ways of working together that were to produce many joint positions on a wide range of subjects, both in relations with other states and within the UN. By 1985 France was ready to accept that the EPC should come closer to the EC, which was stated in the Single European Act.

The next formal development of foreign policy cooperation was its incorporation in the Maastricht Treaty alongside the EC, as the 'second pillar' of the EU. The prospect of German unification had alarmed the French, who feared that the larger Germany might downgrade the Franco-German partnership and pursue an autonomous Eastern policy. Just as they promoted the single currency to anchor Germany in the Community, so they wanted a common foreign policy to limit German autonomy in relations with the East; the Germans, far from opposing this, saw it as part of the design for a Europe united on federal lines; and both President Mitterrand and Chancellor Kohl saw a common foreign policy together with the single currency as cementing permanent peace in Europe (Figure 11). So they proposed the IGC on 'political union' to run in parallel with the one on economic and monetary union.

When Mrs Thatcher asked them what they meant by political union, she got no clear answer. One reason was that, while both were agreed on the idea of a common foreign policy, which was one of the two specific things to which the term was applied, they disagreed about reform of the institutions, which was the other: the French wanted to strengthen the intergovernmental elements, in particular the European Council; the Germans wanted to move towards a federal system by strengthening the Parliament. So they could hardly speak with one voice about it.

11. Kohl and Mitterrand hold hands at Verdun cemetery where a million French and German soldiers are buried.

Thatcher wanted neither and, though she accepted the existing EPC, she did not want the EC institutions to have a hand in it. While Germany envisaged that foreign policy would move towards becoming a Community competence, France too opposed the idea; and the outcome was the intergovernmental 'second pillar' for the Common Foreign and Security Policy (CFSP).

The CFSP was given a grander name than the EPC and more elaborate institutions. Following Europe's poor showing in the Gulf War, defence was mentioned in the treaty, but in ambiguous terms to accommodate both the French desire for an autonomous European defence capacity and British opposition to any such thing, for fear it could weaken Nato. So nothing much resulted from the use of the word 'defence'. Nor indeed did the CFSP produce notably better results than had the EPC before it. So there was a second try, in the Amsterdam Treaty, to devise a satisfactory second pillar.

Amsterdam clarified a number of aspects, including a set of general objectives for CFSP and the possibility of using QMV in some cases, as well as enhanced cooperation. Of more consequence was an attempt to provide for a simpler system of external representation, with the creation of a high representative, a role to be filled by the secretary general of the Council of Ministers Secretariat (i.e. an intergovernmental post). Coupled to increased planning capabilities within the Secretariat, this allowed the High Representative, former Nato Secretary-General Javier Solana, to build a much stronger profile in international organizations.

However, Amsterdam and the minor tinkerings of Nice were still insufficient to address the continuing structural problems that CFSP has faced, and so the Laeken process explicitly focused on the need to engage in a more fundamental reorganization of external representation (see Figure 12). This eventually led to the Lisbon Treaty, which ended the Maastricht pillar system and tried to create a single external figure. This new post, the High Representative for the EU for Foreign Affairs and Security Policy, was to join together the Commission and the Council of Ministers: the individual would be a vice-president of the former and a chair of the latter's foreign affairs formation, as well as attending European Councils. In brief, the High Representative had the potential to become a key international political player, especially with the resources of a new European External Action Service—essentially a European diplomatic corps—behind him or her. Using the legal framework of the Council of Ministers' common positions and joint actions, there was great scope to articulate a distinctively European position in the world.

While the reorganization has helped reduce some of the previous complexity and duplication of the system, it would also be fair to say that the choices to date for the High Representative—first Catherine Ashton and then Federica Mogherini—also indicated the continuing limits that national leaders have sought to impose.

12. How the EU is represented for Common Foreign and Security Policy.

Both individuals have found themselves more occupied with managing the structures of the system than in conspicuous action. Indeed, the dual institutional roles have led as much to a division of focus as to a uniting of policy.

The progressive consolidation of external representation is likely to continue, especially once the new institutions are able to bed in and develop their corporate identities. The growing role for the European Parliament in influencing budget allocations will also surely play a role in this. But it will be in the field of security that the most notable consequences are likely to be felt.

Security

Awareness that the EU should provide more effective military backing for its common policy in former Yugoslavia spurred governments to strengthen its capacity in the field of defence. While recognizing that they depend on Nato and the US for defence against any major threat to their security, they used somewhat stronger language on the EU's own capacity in the Amsterdam Treaty than at Maastricht, envisaging 'the progressive framing of a common defence policy, which might lead to a common defence', the immediate purpose of which was to include humanitarian tasks, peacekeeping, and 'crisis management, including peacemaking'.

This agreement over Nato's role was hard-won, in the face of those countries that wished to keep the US out of the picture, the most notable exponent of which was France. It took the difficult experiences of the conflicts in the Balkans, especially in Kosovo, to demonstrate that Europeans, though their defence expenditure amounted to two-thirds that of the Americans, were capable of delivering only one-tenth of the firepower; and their influence over the conduct of the action was correspondingly limited. This brought together the British and the French, who had made the principal European contribution, to launch their defence initiative. Experience in the Gulf and the Balkan wars had shown the French that they had to come closer to Nato if they were to make an effective military contribution, while the British for their part had come to see the merit of working with the French; and, having declined to become a founder member of the Eurozone, the government saw defence as a field in which a central role for Britain in the EU could be secured.

The result was the joint proposal for an EU rapid reaction force 'up to' 50,000–60,000 strong, which was adopted by the European Council in Helsinki in December 1999; and it was agreed to integrate the Western European Union (WEU) into the EU: this latter had been set up in the late 1940s to provide mutual defence, a role that was largely rolled over to Nato. The EU began to develop the European Security and Defence Policy (ESDP, now referred to as the Common Security and Defence Policy (CSDP)) as the security arm of the CFSP. It established an EU defence planning and staff structure, with Council of Ministers meetings in which defence ministers participate along with the foreign ministers, the Military Committee representing member states' 'defence chiefs', and military staff within the Council of Ministers Secretariat; and it converted the Political Committee, responsible to the Council of Ministers, into the Political and Security Committee. Preparations proceeded for establishing a rapid reaction force, to undertake peacekeeping and crisis management autonomously, 'where Nato as a whole is not engaged', though Nato (which in practice meant American) facilities such as air transport and satellite-based intelligence would usually be required; and this required American consent to any substantial operations. Thus the British government's fears about weakening Nato were allayed; and all member states, including Austria, Finland, Ireland, and Sweden, with their traditions of neutrality, were reassured by the provisions that any member state can opt out of, or into, any action. The Lisbon Treaty reaffirmed these goals, putting CSDP under the control of the High Representative.

This illustrates the difficulties confronting the EU's defence capacity. A critical mass of member states must agree to an action before it can be undertaken; for substantial operations that require Nato facilities and hence American consent, the Americans may not agree to what Europeans want to do, which would give rise to tensions within Nato; and where a European critical mass and American agreement are both available, the intergovernmental arrangements may be too weak to devise and manage a successful operation. While Nato's system is also intergovernmental, American hegemonic leadership has caused it to work. There is no hegemon

A great civilian power ... and more—or less?

among the member states; and while this makes it more feasible to develop the EU as a working democracy, it will at the same time make an intergovernmental system in the field of defence hard to operate.

The EU's development in a field so sensitive to sovereignty can hardly be expected to run smoothly. But it encountered rougher waters following al-Qaeda's terrorist attack on the US in September 2001, when relationships between states were disrupted both in Nato and within the EU itself. The Americans adopted a more unilateralist approach, with the 'war on terror', accompanied by the intervention in Iraq in March 2003; and the EU's member states were sharply divided, with the British, Italian, Polish, and Spanish governments leading the support for the American intervention, while the French and Germans, shortly to be joined by the Italians and Spaniards after changes of government, led those against it. This might have been expected to obstruct the continued development of the EU's capacity in the field of military security as well as relationships within Nato; and it did delay progress of the ESDP for a while. But the EU continued to develop its capacity in the field of security and has now deployed a considerable number of missions in Europe and Africa, suggesting that there is a role for the EU in this arena.

As the EU develops its capacity in the field of security, it will become something more than a great civilian power. But its strength in the economic, environmental, and other aspects of external policy, somewhat condescendingly called 'soft power', is already very important, and has great further potential as a force for the development of a safer and more prosperous world.

Chapter 9
The EU and the rest
of Europe

A most impressive aspect of the EU project has been its ability
to develop and expand from a small group of relatively similar
states in Western Europe into a union of much greater width
and depth. The process of deepening and widening since the
1950s, with its synergies and contradictions, has been recounted
in Chapter 2. Within this long process of enlargement, it is the
expansion into Central and Eastern Europe that has, apart from
de Gaulle's reaction to the British application, been the most
contentious. While member states generally agreed that Eastern
enlargement was to be welcomed, to extend the area of prosperity
and security, there have also been greatly varying degrees of
enthusiasm, to the point where discussion of 'enlargement fatigue'
became not uncommon in the old member states. Certainly,
there have been problems on the way, but enlargement can be
seen as an essential part of the EU and its continued development,
not least in its dealings with those who remain outside; and the
treaty still affirms that membership is open to any European state
that respects 'the principles of liberty, democracy, respect for
human rights and fundamental freedoms, and the rule of law'.

Enlargement to almost all of Western Europe

There is a routine for the process of enlargement. When an
application is received, the Council of Ministers asks the

Commission for its 'Opinion', on the basis of which the Council of Ministers may, unanimously, approve a mandate for negotiations. The Commission negotiates, supervised by the Council of Ministers; and an eventual treaty of accession has to be adopted by unanimity in the Council of Ministers and with the assent of the Parliament, followed by ratification by all the member states.

Membership can be preceded by a form of association. The original example was the Treaty of Association between Greece and the EEC in 1962, which provided for the removal of trade barriers over a transitional period, various forms of cooperation, and a council of association. It also envisaged eventual membership; and after various vicissitudes, Greece did indeed become a member in 1981.

Portugal and Spain were not eligible for association in the 1960s. Their regimes were incompatible with the EC, for which only democratic countries were suitable partners; and Portugal had already in 1960 become a founder member of the Efta, which Britain had promoted in reaction to the establishment of the EEC and which, being confined to a purely trading relationship, was not so concerned about the political complexion of its members. So when democracy replaced dictatorship in the 1970s, both Iberian countries negotiated entry into the EEC without any prior form of association. This was one reason why the negotiations were protracted, with entry achieved only in 1986. Protectionist resistance, from French farmers in particular, was, however, more significant.

The path to membership was different for the more northerly members of Efta. The British, Danes, Norwegians, Swedes, and Swiss had eschewed the political implications of EC membership; and the Austrians were precluded by their post-Second World War declaration of neutrality. Britain, Denmark, and Ireland joined in 1973 without having been associated in any way. Bilateral free trade agreements were at the same time concluded between the EEC and each of the other Efta states, which by then included Iceland; and they were later signed with Finland, which joined Efta in 1986, and Liechtenstein, in 1991.

As soon as the Soviet constraint was removed in 1989, Austria applied for EC membership. Finland, Norway, Sweden, and Switzerland were not far behind. Delors, hoping to delay such enlargement lest it dilute the Community, devised a proposal for the EEA to include the Efta countries with the EC in an extended single market. But the governments of those five did not want to be excluded from decision-taking in the EC, so they all applied for membership, which Austria, Finland, and Sweden achieved in 1995, after a short negotiation facilitated by their existing free trade relationship. Norwegians rejected accession in their referendum and Swiss voters refused to accept even the EEA. So Switzerland continues with its bilateral free trade agreement and only a vestigial EEA remains, associating Norway, Iceland, and Liechtenstein with the EU.

Enlargement to the East

Throughout the Cold War, relations were cool between the EC and the Soviet Union. The Soviet Union refused to accord the EC legal recognition, seeing it as strengthening the 'capitalist camp'; and the EC refused to negotiate with Comecon, the economic organization dominated by the Soviet Union. Following 1989 and the dissolution of the Soviet bloc, Central and Eastern European countries turned towards the EC, which they saw as a bastion of prosperity, democracy, and protection from a chaotic (and collapsing) Soviet Union. They naturally envisaged membership.

The simplest case was the German Democratic Republic (GDR), as the Soviet-controlled part of Germany had called itself. The GDR became part of the Federal Republic of Germany in 1990;

and the EC made the necessary technical adjustments at speed so that the enlarged Germany could assume German membership without delay.

For the other countries of Central and Eastern Europe, extensive aid and development packages were put together under the Commission's leadership. Projects such as PHARE (Poland and Hungary: Assistance in Restructuring their Economies) sought to provide assistance with economic and political restructuring for the emergent democracies, spending roughly €600 million per year between 1990 and 2003, when it was wound up. However, such assistance, while welcome, was seen by many in the region as a diversion from membership. Indeed, such a view was an accurate reflection of the ambivalence felt by many EU members about enlargement. While publicly proclaiming the historic mission of the EU to reunite Europe peacefully, many politicians were concerned about the admission of a large number of relatively poor, relatively small, and relatively unstable new members, whose populations might then move en masse to the West in order to find employment.

It was only in 1993, at the Copenhagen European Council, that the EU agreed the principle of offering full membership to those who wanted it. However, the EU also agreed for the first time to expand on the provisions of the treaty and laid out what became known as 'the Copenhagen criteria': stable democracy, human rights and protection of minorities, the rule of law, a competitive market economy, and the 'ability to take on the obligations of membership including adherence to the aims of political, economic and monetary union'. While political union meant different things in different member states, the significance of 'the obligations of membership' was clear enough, including the huge task of applying not far short of 100,000 pages of legislation, mostly concerning the single market. To allay fears that widening would result in weakening, there was also the condition that the EU should have 'the capacity to absorb new members while maintaining the momentum of integration'.

Despite this laying out of the threshold for membership, and the development of extensive programmes of assistance to the states of Central and Eastern Europe in order to help them meet it, it was only after the conclusion of the Amsterdam Treaty in 1997 that things really started to move. In 1998, the EU judged that a first wave of five had made the necessary progress, so negotiations began in 1998 with the Czech Republic, Estonia, Hungary, Poland, and Slovenia, as well as Cyprus, which had also applied to join; and a second wave, in 2000, comprising Bulgaria, Latvia, Lithuania, Romania, and Slovakia, as well as Malta. While the EU had indicated that each individual accession negotiation would proceed at its own speed, it was agreed at the 2003 Copenhagen European Council that all save Bulgaria and Romania would be able to join in May 2004. These two were able to become members in 2007 (Map 2).

The process of enlargement to the East was very protracted, for a number of reasons. On the part of the new member states, the adjustments required were very substantial, especially within the context of emerging from Communist, planned economy systems. Many states simply lacked the institutions, resources, or experience necessary to implement fundamental changes in the operation of many areas of public policy and decision-making. On the part of the existing member states, we have already mentioned the fears about the increased heterogeneity of the EU and implications of free movement and of the state of EU policies. This last point was to take up much of the EU's time in the late 1990s, as it struggled to reform CAP and cohesion policies to cope with the imminent arrival of a large number of poor states with significant agricultural sectors: those reforms are discussed in Chapter 5. Seen broadly, the solution that was found was to reform the policies by changing the types of support provided, but also to limit the amount that new states could claim in any case. Such an apparently unfair approach to new members has been a consistent feature of all previous enlargements, as existing members seek to protect their interests while they can with applicant states having

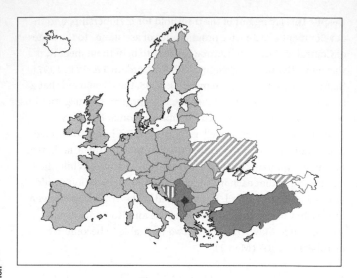

Current EU member States

Candidate States (Albania, Macedonia, Montenegro, Serbia, Turkey)

Application submitted (Bosnia & Herzegovina)

Potential Candidate States (Kosovo)

States with EU Association Agreements, including an intention for membership (Georgia, Moldova, Ukraine)

Map 2. Candidates for future accession.

as yet little leverage to fight it. This was also evident with the discussions about institutional reform that culminated in the Nice Treaty, which a number of member states found unsatisfactory enough to call for the constitutional convention.

For all of this concern, perhaps the most remarkable feature of the post-enlargement EU is how unproblematic it has been to date. Despite the delay in replacing the Nice settlement with that of Lisbon, the EU's decision-making bodies have functioned without undue problems arising from the enlargement, and the gridlock that some had predicted in the 1990s has not come to pass. Indeed, when we consider the most obvious crises within the EU, these have been more about old member states than new ones: the French and Dutch 'no' votes on the Constitutional Treaty; the Anglo-French split over the Iraq War and its aftermath; Greece's membership of the euro; Brexit. While the immigration crisis has been a counter-point to this, with stiff opposition from Hungary and Poland, there has not been the emergence of any clear 'old' and 'new' Europe cleavage in the EU. Instead it has been the cross-cutting issues of economics, democracy, and identity that have shaped the way the EU has developed.

South-Eastern Europe

Before it disintegrated, the former Yugoslavia had been closer to the EC than had any other Central or Eastern European state. Then came the disintegration and the wars. The US initially wanted the Europeans to deal with the problems. Jacques Poos, Luxembourg's Foreign Minister and President-in-Office of the Council of Ministers in the first half of 1991, famously said 'This is the hour of Europe'. Slovenia secured independence without much fighting, but bitter wars ensued in Croatia, Bosnia, and later in Kosovo, and in all three cases the EU failed completely to match Poos's claim. Instead, it was the US and Nato that were the main actors in securing a durable peace settlement in the region, the EU being relegated to providing humanitarian relief.

The key consequence of this for the EU was to stimulate a complete review of the Common Foreign and Security Policy, most notably with the creation of hard military capabilities in order to secure the so-called Petersberg tasks of humanitarian relief, peacekeeping, and crisis management. It also helped to make the EU consider how its various external policies linked together, most obviously seen in the creation of the High Representative to give a single face to the EU's work. As far as the Balkans were concerned, the result of the EU's initial failure was a return to the drawing board and the production of a Stability Pact for South-Eastern Europe. This overarching set of policies, designed to strengthen democracy, human rights, and economic reform, was later followed by Stability and Association Agreements between the EU and each of the West Balkan states. This is backed by the EU's Instrument for Pre-Accession Assistance, which provides the West Balkans with some €500 million per year. With the slow stabilization of the region, the EU has been able to offer membership to Croatia; full candidate status to Albania, Macedonia, Montenegro, and Serbia; and a provisional status to the others with Stability and Association Agreements, thus providing a strong incentive for local politicians to follow the example of the other Central and Eastern Europeans.

Russia and the Commonwealth of Independent States

The three Baltic republics of the former Soviet Union, Estonia, Latvia, and Lithuania, declined to join Russia in the successor Commonwealth of Independent States (CIS) and became EU members in 2004. Among the states that stayed with the CIS, six could claim to be European: Armenia, Belarus, Georgia, Moldova, Ukraine, and Russia itself. They could therefore, if they came to fulfil the conditions of stable democracy and competitive market economy, apply for membership of the EU.

As the EU has expanded to the borders of Russia and Ukraine, the question of inclusion of the CIS states has been raised. The size and hostility of Russia, however, combined with its much greater economic and political disparities with the EU than those found in Central and Eastern Europe, stand in the way. The policy has therefore been to develop closer bilateral and multilateral relations rather than to envisage membership. The other states too face great difficulties: the conflict in Ukraine from 2014 was driven in part by profound disagreement on the desirability of a membership path and the implications for their relationship with Russia. At the very least, this makes membership little more than a long-term possibility (Map 3).

The EU has, however, long been eager to help with the transition to democracy and free market economics throughout the CIS. From 1991 until 2007, the EU operated a very extensive programme of assistance known as Technical Assistance to the Commonwealth of Independent States (TACIS). This concentrated on such things as enterprise restructuring and development, administrative reform, social services, education, and, as the biggest item, nuclear safety, which accounts for a large part of the regional programmes. However, as will be seen in Chapter 10, TACIS has now been superseded by the European Neighbourhood Policy.

The EU's relationship with Russia remains an ambiguous one. While the military rivalry of the Cold War has largely gone, the uncertain nature of Russian democracy under Vladimir Putin in the new century has created new points of tension. The more aggressive stance taken in its diplomacy—not to mention its actions, including the annexation of Crimea in 2014—suggest that despite the continuing reliance on Russian energy sources for many EU states, there is almost no scope for building more enhanced links beyond the current Partnership and Cooperation Agreement. Indeed, the growing concerns about Russia as a security threat have tended to push the EU back towards a stance not so far from the one held during the Cold War: relatively low in trust, and focused more on the risks than any potential benefits. Until Putin leaves office that is unlikely to change.

The European Union

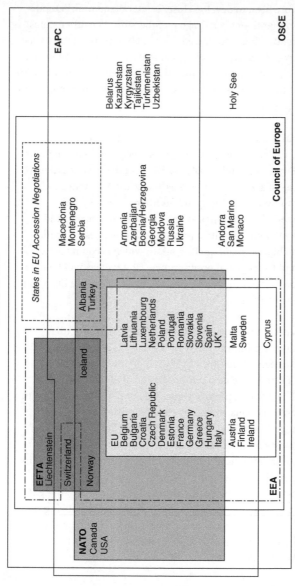

EAPC = Euro-Atlantic Partnership Council; EEA = European Economic Area; EFTA = European Free Trade Area; EU = European Union; NATO = North Atlantic Treaty Organization; OSCE = Organization for Security and Co-operation in Europe. * the UK notified the EU in 2017 of its intention to withdraw.

Map 3. The architecture of Europe, 2017.

Turkey

We cannot complete this chapter without reference to Turkey. Just as Russia is a problematic partner for the EU, so too has Turkey become ever more of a thorn in its side.

Turkey concluded a Treaty of Association with the EEC in 1964—like that of Greece, save that the EC's doubts about Turkey were reflected in a transition period of twenty-two years and no clear commitment to membership. Turkey lodged its application for membership in 1987, but it was not until 1999 that the EU recognized it as a candidate, and negotiations began only in 2005, with accession not expected for many years yet. Even by EU standards, such a protracted process requires some explanation.

EU politicians have voiced a number of reasons for doubting whether Turkey should become a member. First, there has been reference to the Copenhagen criteria and the country's unsuitability on the grounds of human rights abuses, the role of the military in politics, weaknesses in the economy, and the extent to which reforms can meaningfully be made. Second, there are concerns regarding the size of Turkey (it would before long be the EU's largest member state, owing to its high birth rate) and the resultant potential for large-scale migration to other member states and voting weight in the Council of Ministers. Third, there has been much talk of 'enlargement fatigue' and the need for a more substantial pause before such a major expansion. Fourth, and perhaps underlining all of these other dimensions, is the notion of Turkey's 'otherness'. As a majority Muslim population, as a state with a tenuous claim to be geographically 'European', and as a state with a very different historical path from that of current members, it challenges many conceptions of what the EU is and should be.

From the Turkish perspective, their persistence in the face of such opposition reflects the strength of the Western Kemalist project in the country and of its self-conception as a bridge between East and West. Certainly, successive Turkish governments have made very extensive modifications to legal and political structures in order to secure the accession negotiations that they so desire, something that is all the more surprising considering the lack of certainty that such negotiations might occur. However, the election of Recep Tayyip Erdogan as Prime Minister and then President has marked something of a sea-change in relations. Erdogan has focused on building up Turkey's profile as a pivot state in its region, coupled with a reaffirmation of moderate Islamist views that have become much less favourable to EU membership. While he was willing to reach an agreement in 2016 with the EU on supporting refugees from Syria and on enforcing stronger border controls on movement towards the EU, this was driven by the access to funds that it provided, rather than any desire to use it as a basis to advance the stalled membership negotiations.

As such, Turkey's membership remains unresolved. In many member states, Turkish membership is deeply problematic, both for publics and elites. However, the question has to be asked of whether excluding Turkey is desirable or not. The EU already has over fifteen million Muslim citizens, so religion is not the barrier that some imagine. Likewise, admitting Turkey could help consolidate the EU's status as a global power, both through the admission of a state that bridges into the Middle East and through its extensive military capability. While the matter might stand in abeyance at present it is not fully a dead letter and it will have serious implications for the EU and its future development.

Chapter 10
The EU in the world

Having shown how 'federal institutions can unite highly
developed states', the EC might serve as an example of how 'to
create a more prosperous and peaceful world'. Such was the hope
that Jean Monnet expressed in 1954 to the students of Columbia
University in New York. The EU has been concerned, like others,
to look after its own interests, even if it is often hard to reach
agreement on what these are. But Europeans have become more
aware than most others that these do include the creation of a
prosperous and peaceful world. How do its actions, as distinct
from its example as a region of peace and welfare, contribute
to that end?

The EC as a great trading power

The US sponsored the uniting of Europe, from Marshall Aid to
the birth and early development of the EC. Monnet reciprocated
with the idea of an increasingly equal EC–US partnership. Soon
after the EEC was founded with its common external tariff, the
US launched the Kennedy Round of trade liberalization in
the Gatt; and this led in 1967, after five years of laborious
negotiations, to the agreement to cut tariffs by one-third.

That would have been out of the question had the EC not become,
with its common tariff as an instrument of external policy, a

trading partner on level terms with the US. As an observer in Washington put it, the EC was 'now the most important member of Gatt', and the key to further efforts to liberalize trade. So it indeed became in later rounds of Gatt negotiations, as the creative American impulse of the post-war period declined. The EC played the leading part in the Uruguay Round, concluded in 1994. With tariffs on most manufactures already low, the focus moved to non-tariff barriers where the single market programme gave the EC a unique experience in techniques of liberalization. Its experience was also relevant to the replacement of the Gatt by the WTO, with its wider scope and greater powers for resolving disputes: a step, perhaps, towards validating the suggestion that the EC's 'example of effective international law-making' might at some stage be 'replicated at global level'.

Of course the EC's trade relations have engendered the normal clash of interests, or at least of what participants suppose to be their interests, with agriculture being the prime bone of contention. The protectionist common agricultural policy damaged trading partners such as Australia, Canada, New Zealand, and the US. Following UK accession, this was particularly harmful to the first three, a blow that could have been avoided had Britain not failed to join when the Rome Treaty was negotiated. It was not until the 1990s that the EU began to carry out serious reform, when it cut the level of protection for some major items by about half; and it was agreed in the Uruguay Round that the trade-disrupting export subsidies would be eliminated in the following round: a tough challenge for both the EU and the US.

While moving closer together on agriculture, the EU and the US diverged over environmental, cultural, and consumer protection issues, with the Europeans favouring standards which led to restriction of their imports from the US and which the Americans regarded as protectionist. Genetically modified organisms, hormone-treated beef, noisy aero-engines, data privacy, and films and television programmes were cases in point.

The friction induced by the EU's network of preferential arrangements has, on the contrary, been eased as tariffs were reduced in successive Gatt rounds. That network had become so extensive, covering almost the whole of Europe and the less well-developed countries, that only a few remained outside it, the latter including Australia, Canada, Japan, New Zealand, South Africa, and the US. The Americans were irked by the EC's preferences for particular countries. But the other side of this coin was the relationships that the EC established with large parts of the world's South, which were, however, put to a hard test in the Doha Round of trade negotiations that opened in 2001, with the EU wanting a comprehensive agenda and the US preferring to concentrate on fields such as agriculture and the environment.

The EU's desire to include matters such as investment, competition policy, public procurement, and trade facilitation, known as the 'Singapore issues', was motivated partly by the view that the world should start moving, as the EU itself had done, beyond the focus on tariffs and import quotas in order to deal with other areas of policy that have a growing impact on trade. But developing countries were not ready for this; and their negotiating power was enhanced by the creation of the G20, led by Brazil, China, India, and South Africa, with others representing regional and trading interests (see Chart 7). Agriculture also emerged, as usual, as an obstacle, with the European and American farm lobbies resisting liberalization; and for some less well-developed countries there was an additional problem arising from the EU's 'everything but arms' decision to abolish restrictions on imports from the forty poorest countries, to the detriment of their competitors in other less well-developed countries.

The continued floundering of the Doha round since then—notwithstanding the agreement in early 2017 of the Trade Facilitation Agreement to cut back on red tape—has meant that there has been a rise in more bilateral or regional activity by all

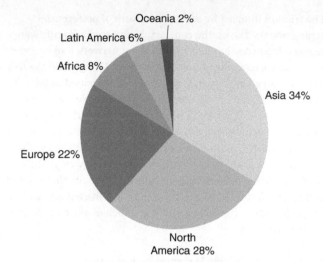

Total exports: €1,790.7 billion

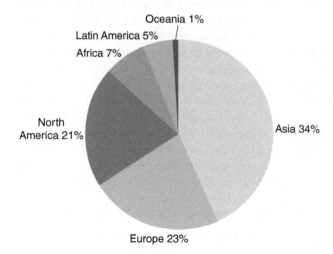

Total imports: €1,726.5 billion

Chart 7. Direction of EU trade by region, 2015.

involved. Whether this is a sustainable or desirable strategy remains to be seen, but in any case the relevance of the EU's experience remains clear.

The EU, its neighbourhood, and the developing world

Whereas relations with the US are important for all member states, individual states have special relationships with particular countries in most of the rest of the world; and many of these became shared by the EU as a whole.

This, like much else, stems from the Treaty of Rome. France wanted advantages for its colonies, and made this a condition for ratification of the treaty. So the EC as a whole granted free entry to imports from these colonies and provided them with aid through the European Development Fund (EDF). The same applied to territories relating to Belgium, Italy, and the Netherlands; and the resulting association was the original basis for the present Cotonou Convention. French pressure also led to preferential agreements for Morocco and Tunisia; and these were the forerunners of the present far-reaching system of agreements with neighbouring states.

After they became independent, the association with former colonies was transmuted through the Convention that provided for joint institutions: the Council of Ministers, Committee of Ambassadors, and Assembly of Parliamentarians. Following British accession, the Commonwealth countries of Africa, the Caribbean, and the Pacific joined in negotiating the Lomé Convention. This broadened the participation to include most of Africa and the Caribbean islands, as well as a number of islands in the Pacific, known collectively as the ACP countries. It removed some vestiges of the colonial system and has expanded the aid towards a level of €3 billion a year since the 1990s, together with money to cushion the associates against falls in their income from commodity exports.

Box 5 Cotonou Convention, 2000–20

The EU and ACP states agreed in 2000 to renew the Lomé Convention for the fifth time, for a twenty-year period. The resultant Cotonou Convention is revised every five years and the aid protocols are also limited to five-year periods. The ACP-EU Council of Ministers meets yearly to review progress.

Trade is at the heart of the agreement. Negotiations between the EU and groups of ACP states for 'economic partnership agreements' are to result eventually in new trading arrangements (Economic Partnership Agreements) intended to lead to an EU-ACP free trade area by 2020. Meanwhile the free or preferential entry to the EU is to be retained.

Aid is set at €30.5 billion for 2014–20, via the EDF. Good performance in the use of aid is to be rewarded.

Poverty reduction is to be a favoured focus for development strategies.

Non-state actors are to be encouraged to participate in the development process.

Political dialogue indicates a harder-nosed EU approach, with good governance, respect for human rights, democratic principles, and the rule of law as criteria for aid policy, and with action against corruption.

Cotonou is coloured by the EU's disappointment with the results of the preceding Lomé I–IV, attributed to poor governance in many countries. Given this starting point, the development of an EU-ACP free trade area is a very ambitious idea and one that has already slipped behind schedule.

The Lomé Convention was renewed for the fifth time at Cotonou in the year 2000, in difficult circumstances (see Box 5). For the associates were disturbed by the erosion of the margins of preference as tariffs had been reduced in successive Gatt rounds; and the EU was concerned that, despite the massive quantities of aid, almost all of Africa remained in bad shape, owing at least partly to poor governance and unstable relations with former colonial powers in the EU. Cotonou sought to answer this with more focus on the development of good governance and of regional cooperation, to provide a more conducive environment for the pursuit of development goals in the seventy-nine ACP partners. Thus issues including human rights and climate change have become key parts of a broad agenda of support and interaction.

By the end of the 1970s the EC also had a network of agreements according preferences and assistance to states around the Mediterranean, with content not unlike that of the Lomé Convention but without the multilateral institutions. This network stretched along the North African coast and up into the Levant states.

By the 1990s, a combination of economic difficulties, political instability, and rapid population growth in most of these countries, with consequent pressure to migrate to Europe, caused growing anxiety in the EU, particularly among its southern states. The outcome was a conference of ministers from the EU and its Mediterranean partners, held in Barcelona in 1995, which launched a 'Euro-Mediterranean process' aimed at building a wide range of multilateral links across the basin. However, the headline goal of the process—a free trade area by 2005—was soon to founder on the political differences of the partners and the constant distraction of the Eastern enlargement (Map 4).

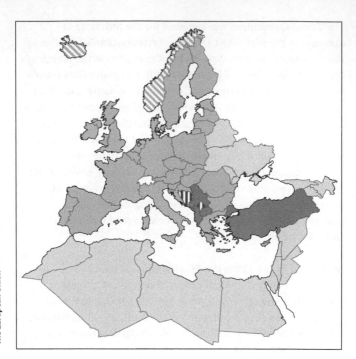

The European Union

□ Current EU member States

■ Candidate States (Albania, Macedonia, Montenegro, Serbia, Turkey)

⊞ Potential Candidate States (Bosnia & Herzegovina, Kosovo)

⊠ Non-EU European Area members (Iceland, Liechtenstein, Norway)

□ European Neighbourhood Policy partners (Algeria, Armenia, Azerbaijan, Belarus, Egypt, Georgia, Israel, Lebanon, Libya, Moldova, Morocco, Palestinian Authority, Syria, Tunisia,Turkey, Ukraine)

Map 4. The EU's neighbourhood.

With the coming of that enlargement, the EU engaged in a wholesale review of its links with its neighbours, with a particular eye on trying to keep the EU an open and accessible grouping. Thus it was in 2003 that the Commission proposed replacing the Euro-Mediterranean process, PHARE, and TACIS with the European Neighbourhood Policy (ENP). In 2007, these former programmes were formally incorporated into the ENP, supported by a new financial instrument that will provide some €1.7 billion a year for cross-border cooperation, the development of civil society, and technical assistance.

While the ENP represented a significant commitment on the part of the EU to these countries, there has been little to show in the way of a more stable, democratic, or prosperous environment around the EU's borders, especially in light of the Arab spring of 2011 and the spillover of the Syrian civil war.

Asia, Latin America, and generalized preferences

Britain, on joining the EC, managed to secure satisfactory terms for Commonwealth countries from Africa, the Caribbean, and the Pacific. But no special arrangement was agreed for the Asian members of the Commonwealth—India, Pakistan (which then included Bangladesh), Sri Lanka, Malaysia, Hong Kong, and Singapore—most of whose exports had entered Britain tariff-free under Commonwealth preference. The damage was limited, however, because in 1971 the EC was among the first to adopt the Generalized System of Preferences (GSP), according preferential entry to imports from almost all Third World countries that did not already benefit from the Lomé Convention or the Mediterranean agreements; and this reduced the discrimination against most Asian and Latin American countries (see Box 6). The system was less favourable than it may sound because for 'sensitive' (i.e. more competitive) products there were quotas limiting the preferences to quantities fixed

Box 6 EU international agreements beyond Cotonou and ENP

The EU has free trade agreements in place with:

Canada	El Salvador	Peru
Chile	Guatemala	South Africa
Colombia	Mexico	South Korea
Costa Rica	Nicaragua	
Ecuador	Panama	

In addition, the EU has concluded agreements with Singapore and Vietnam, and is in negotiations with Argentina, Brazil, India, Indonesia, Japan, Malaysia, New Zealand, Paraguay, Philippines, Thailand, and Uruguay.

The EU has links with other regional groupings, including:

Andean Community (Latin America)	SAARC (South Asian Association for Regional Co-operation)
Mercosur (Latin America)	SADC (South African Development Community)
San José group (Central America)	ASEAN
Gulf Co-operation Council	

The EU's Generalized System of Preferences applies to almost all Third World countries.

in advance for each product and each member state. But the generalized preferences nevertheless helped to strengthen links with less well-developed countries.

While the margins of preference that the GSP affords less well-developed countries have declined along with the reduction of the general level of tariffs, their links with the EU through its aid programmes have become increasingly important. These amount to some €10 billion a year, including both humanitarian aid and the development aid for ACP countries and the ENP. The EU has also concluded bilateral trade and cooperation agreements to strengthen its links with major developing countries, including India, Mexico, and Brazil; it has agreements with regional groups such as ASEAN (the Association of South-East Asian Nations); and since Portugal and Spain joined the EC in 1986, their special links with Latin America have been added to those of other member states in Africa and Asia (see Charts 8 and 9).

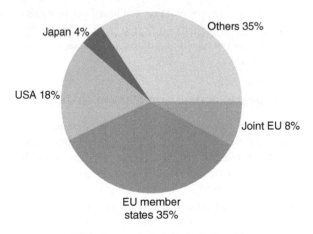

NB: This does not include humanitarian aid

Chart 8. Shares of official development aid from the EU, the US, Japan, and others (2014).

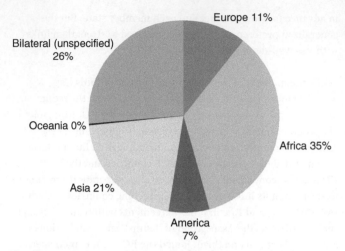

Chart 9. **Development aid from the EU and member states by destination, 2014.**

While the economic impact of the agreements, preferences, and aid can hardly be measured and may not have been very great, the EU has gained political credit which may be of help in the future development of its relationships with Asian, African, and Latin American countries.

Security: peacekeeping and climate change

American hegemony in defence will, however, remain unchallenged for as long ahead as can be contemplated. Not only would Europeans have to undertake vast expenditure in any attempt to become independent of American strategic power, but the force thus acquired would also have to be controlled by a solidly established democratic European state with a number of years of reliable decision-taking behind it. So Europeans continue to depend on Nato's American-led strategic shield; and their efforts in the field of defence will be mainly to contribute to peacekeeping and peacemaking, particularly in actions sponsored by the UN. For defence of the EU's territory against major threats, Europeans will continue to depend on American protection.

It would be unwise to assume that such protection would never be needed, in what is becoming a multipolar world in strategic as well as economic terms, and where a growing number of states have weapons of mass destruction. Military threats to the EU's interests could, moreover, emerge with which the Americans may be unable or unwilling to deal, especially following the election of Donald Trump. So the EU is likely to continue building its defence capacity as well as keeping the alliance in repair, while at the same time using its soft power to further the development of a safer world.

The EU did, as we saw in Chapter 8, resume the development of its military activities without much delay, following the internal divisions during the build-up to the American intervention in Iraq. In 2003, the European Council unanimously approved an EU strategy to strengthen security around the EU and in the international order. In 2004, the Nato force in Bosnia was replaced by an EU force of 7,000 troops, with Nato assets and capabilities; and smaller but significant operations were undertaken in Georgia, Macedonia, and the Democratic Republic of Congo—the latter a precursor of the project for establishing battle groups which was launched in the same year. By 2006, the EU sent a peacekeeping force of some 8,000 troops to Lebanon after the war there between Hizbollah and Israel. Since 2008, the EU has also provided substantial resources to combating piracy in Somalia with its Atalanta mission.

Thus the EU continued creating a significant capacity for military contributions to peacekeeping and peacemaking, a most important complement to which is its capacity to contribute to the civilian elements of peacekeeping, together with its experience in assisting the building of democratic states. One example, which can follow directly from a successful military mission, is the police missions, such as those provided by the EU in Bosnia, where in 2003 the EU took over from a UN Police Task Force, followed by others in Macedonia, Democratic Republic of Congo, and Palestinian Territories. More broadly, it has much experience in assisting with the development of political, judicial, and administrative institutions, and the structures of civil society, particularly among Central and Eastern European states preparing themselves for accession, as well as in the West Balkans and farther afield; and this has great potential importance for wider application in a world in which failed or failing states can be a serious security risk, while solidly based democracies can contribute much to stable international relations.

The environment is also a vital aspect of security, with climate change representing one of the gravest threats to the welfare, and perhaps the lives, of the world's people; and the EU has made the major contribution to international efforts to deal with it. In 1986, when it had become evident that chlorofluorocarbons (CFCs) could destroy the ozone layer and thus endanger life on Earth, the EC succeeded in breaking a deadlock in negotiations for the Montreal Protocol to the UN Framework Convention on Climate Change (UNFCCC), thus halting the degradation. Then in 1997 the EU played the leading part in the negotiations for the UNFCCC's Kyoto Protocol to stem the emissions of carbon dioxide and other greenhouse gases, which are generating a potentially disastrous degree of global warming. After much disagreement on the approach this embodied, the EU was also a key player in the 2015 Paris Agreement, which aims to hold global average temperatures below 2 per cent of pre-industrial levels, via a system of nationally determined contributions. Having concluded that global emissions need to be cut by 60 per cent by mid-century and having adopted that target for its own emissions, the EU has a compelling interest in securing similar commitments from as many states as possible.

The EU's role in the world

Too much American hegemony is dangerous for Americans as well as for others. Overwhelming power can lead to rash decisions; and the burden is too great for one country to carry alone. China seems likely to catch up with the US during the first half of this century as a military as well as economic power, with unpredictable consequences; and India may well follow. But the EU has the potential to be, much sooner, at least an equal partner with the US with respect to the economy, the environment, and soft security, though not defence (Figure 13).

Indeed, the EU's long-standing parity with the US in the world trading system has shown what can be done when sufficiently effective institutions dispose of a common instrument. The euro offers a basis for a similar performance in the international monetary system, if the institutions for external monetary policy are adequately reformed. For action on global climate change the EU should be able, again with some strengthening of its institutions, to maintain its leading role. Soft security—the use of economic, social, and cultural elements of international action, including the civilian aspects of keeping the peace—is a field in which it is developing a capacity that could become an essential counterpart for American military power; and the military instruments that the EU is creating also open up opportunities to perform a complementary role.

Adjustment to such changes in power relationships is always hard for those who have been on top. But it should not be too hard for Americans to adjust to a more powerful EU, with a society that shares so much in so many ways; with four decades of reasonable cooperation in the field of trade where both already have equivalent strength; and with no prospect of rivalry in the field of military power. Having adjusted to an equal partnership with the EU in most other fields, it should be easier for the US to

13. The informal meeting of the Union's leaders in Bratislava in September 2016, to discuss the future of the EU; the UK was not invited.

adjust to changes in relationships with other emergent powers, particularly as the EU will be well-placed, with its network of relations with countries around the world, to advance the process of creating a stable world system that accommodates them.

The EU's own experience of institutions, policies, and attitudes that have helped the member states to live together in peace for half a century, together with its worldwide network of relationships, should indeed enable it to influence others to move in a similar direction. But Monnet's idea that such institutions might serve to create a prosperous and peaceful world could be realized only under quite exacting conditions. The necessary sharing of sovereignty is possible only among pluralist democracies that are willing to accept a common rule of law, and have the capacity to develop common legislative institutions to enact it and a system of government to implement policies within it. These conditions apply to a large extent within the EU, but in many parts of the world they do not. Meanwhile the EU can assist efforts to develop such conditions where they do not yet exist and to undertake EU-type developments where they do; and it can support steps to help the UN and other international organizations to become more effective, while recognizing that institutions of an EU type cannot be created at that level until pluralist democracy becomes the norm throughout the world. But EU policies which point towards such an outcome are in the long-term interest of its states and citizens; and even if a very long time-scale has to be envisaged, the European experience has shown that initiating a process which leads in that direction can already begin to transform relations between states.

Chapter 11
Much accomplished...but what next?

The paradox of the EU might be neatly summed up by the events at the end of March 2017, when the latest edition of this work was being finalized. On one side, the celebrations of the sixtieth anniversary of the signing of the treaties of Rome were an opportunity to reflect on the extent to which the process of integration has become a fundamental part of European governance and government, reaching into almost every area of public policy and stretching further across the continent than any might have imagined at its start. On the other, just a few days later, the submission of the UK's intention to withdraw from the EU was made: the start of a process that will take years to complete, but which has already changed the landscape for those activists unhappy with the way the EU works. In those two events, we can see both the achievement and the fragility of the system that has been built up since the 1950s.

Therefore it needs to be asked not only whether the EU has the necessary powers and structures to achieve its objectives, but also whether its objectives are the right ones in the first place. Without considering the latter, the former risks becoming an exercise in political narcissism.

Do the powers and instruments match the aims?

We might begin by observing that the EU has been able to achieve its aims where it has the powers and instruments as well as the institutions with which to act. The powers and instruments can be legislative, such as the framework for the single market; fiscal, as with the budget or the common external tariff; or financial, as with the aid programmes or the single currency. Cooperation based on the powers and instruments of member states can be useful, but would not achieve much without the hard core of common powers and instruments.

The single market legislation provides a framework for a high level of economic integration, even if it remains incomplete in some significant sectors and will need continued development; and, for member states that have adopted the euro, the single currency completes the single market in the monetary domain.

The budget has transferred resources to sectors deemed to require support, originally to agriculture but increasingly to less well-developed regions and member states. While the agricultural budget has generated conflict, the structural funds to assist development of poorer regions have been more generally favoured, as has the support for research and economic modernization.

Thus the EU has many of the necessary powers in the economic field. The same can be said in the field of the environment, where the need for both internal and external action to limit the damage from climate change remains a long-term priority.

Social policy as embodied in the welfare state belongs largely, following the principle of subsidiarity, to the member states. That principle justifies EU involvement in some employment-related aspects of social policy, such as the prevention of social dumping by undercutting standards of health and safety at work. There is a grey area, including elements of social security and hours of work, where there is conflict between those who want to establish EU-wide standards and those who consider that differences rooted in varying social cultures should not be disturbed. Disagreements remain; but the latter view has gained ground.

While the economic and environmental aims and powers were promoted by interest groups as well as federalists, as was the free movement of workers across the internal frontiers, it was the federal idea that lay behind free movement for all within the EU. Notwithstanding the partial suspension of Schengenland provisions, the centrality of free movement has ended up being underlined by the UK's move to leave the EU, as member states reflect on the core ideas of their integration. Indeed, it is telling that all member states participate in measures to combat cross-frontier crime, whatever their views on other matters; even the British government seems to desire to be involved in this, despite leaving the organization.

In the field of its external relations, the EU's powers have been designed to defend and promote common interests, which include stability in the international economic and political system. The most potent instrument is the offer of accession, hence of participation in the EU's institutions and powers as a whole. However, as well as only being available for European states, the distinct lack of political interest in further enlarging the EU has made this a less credible tool in recent years.

The powers over external trade, together with the instrument of the common external tariff, have enabled the EU to serve its interest in liberal international trade as well as to turn what was American hegemony in this field into an EU–US partnership. The protectionist common agricultural policy, working in the opposite direction, marred relations with many trading partners.

Reforms to correct this distortion have taken far too long, but are being accomplished by stages. A combination of preferential arrangements and aid has strengthened links with most Third World countries.

Along with this influence in the world trading system, the EU has used its environmental powers to play a leading part in international negotiations to protect the ozone layer and to limit damage from climate change. Similarly, the EU has continued to be a central part of the system of international development and post-conflict reconstruction and support, forming a major pillar of the architecture of global governance.

The institutions: how effective? how democratic?

Eurosceptic discourse has tended to regard 'closer integration' as undesirable without distinguishing between transfer of powers to the EU and reform of its institutions. But these are two very different questions. The transfer of powers is justified only where the EU can serve its citizens in ways that individual member states cannot; and the EU already has many of the powers indicated by the subsidiarity principle except in the field of defence. Once powers have been transferred, however, they will not serve citizen interests well enough unless they are wielded by effective and democratic EU institutions.

The political institutions require a context of the rule of law, which is ensured by the Court of Justice in matters of EU competence; and this has brought fundamental change in the relations among member states.

The Council of Ministers' shift towards qualified majority voting in most areas of activity has not only permitted a more efficient and effective decision-making process, but has also reflected the building levels of trust that member states have in the joint decisions that are reached. While there remain some areas where unanimity continues to be required, these are in matters of particular sensitivity—enlargement or third-country agreements—which find themselves increasingly subsumed into a broader pattern of cooperative activity in which the Council of Ministers acts as a permanent clearing house for interactions and understandings between member states. In short, the reflex in most European capitals is to look to Brussels as a space for debate and cooperation on many matters of public policy.

The Commission has substantial powers to fulfil its functions as the EU's executive, though its role in ensuring that member states do in fact carry out the administration that is delegated to them by the EU is not strong enough, and too much intervention by the Council of Ministers and its network of committees in the execution of EU decisions hampers the Commission's effectiveness. As an institution, the Commission looks set to continue operating within the limits set out by the member states, rather than exerting the kind of leadership seen in its early days.

The Parliament tends to carve its own path, as seen with the *Spitzenkandidaten* initiative in 2014, but its powers are still constrained by the treaties. The Lisbon Treaty did make co-decision into (literally) the Ordinary Legislative Procedure, reflecting its general application. But there still remain assorted Special Legislative Procedures and, for as long as these remain, the EU will be neglecting an essential means of securing citizen support. Even with their strengthened rights under the Lisbon Treaty, citizens still lack a meaningful connection with the EU; and it would be unwise to ignore the track record of representative democracy as a major element in citizenship. As long as citizens do not see the Parliament as being on an equal footing with the Council of Ministers, they are not likely to regard it as a sufficiently important channel of representation. The Council of Ministers, representing the states, is an essential part of the EU's legislature too. But despite the progress in holding legislative sessions in public, it remains at the centre of an opaque system of quasi-diplomatic negotiation. Representation in a powerful house of the citizens may well be a condition of the latter's support for the EU over the longer term.

The success of the provision for gender equality at work shows how citizens' rights can also generate support for the EU. The incorporation of the Charter of Fundamental Rights provides some positives, but more important will be the EU's general effectiveness in doing things that are necessary for citizens. It must be seen to be doing such things at a time when it confronts major challenges, both internally and in the world at large.

The UK's decision to leave the EU has shown, in the starkest of ways, the limits to popular support that the EU's model has encountered throughout its development. As much as there have been particularly British elements in the mix—the nature of media coverage, the strength of the idea of the country as 'of, but not in' Europe (to recall Churchill's words)—it is vital to note that the UK is different in degree rather than in nature from other states.

This is seen on both the demand and the supply sides of the debate in the 2016 referendum. People struggled to see the benefits of integration—economic growth and development, enhanced security, social and environmental protection—while the costs loomed large: the latter included not only what was felt to be a problematic level of long- and short-term migration into the UK, but also a feeble Eurozone and a general sense that the EU had become an ineffectual organization. Similarly, those politicians who had long blamed 'Brussels' for unpopular decisions now found it hard to make the case for cooperation with other member states, even as the EU itself seemed to lack the power to deal with its long list of problems.

Perhaps the final element in this is the long-standing paradox that the benefits of integration have tended to be spread very widely and so tend to be little noticed, while the costs are much more concentrated. Thus most people tend to notice the ease of moving freely across borders on the occasions that they go on holiday—when they also can benefit from cheaper mobile phone charges and cleaner beaches—while those exposed to the increased competition of an integrated European market might find their entire livelihood swept away.

Underpinning all of this has been a failure of political debate across the EU, a failure to have a mature and frank discussion about the compromises and trade-offs involved in the process. While there are substantial benefits to be gained from working together, this is not without cost, and the reflex of national politicians to claim for the benefits even as they push the costs onto a 'foreign' (in both senses) EU could never be a sustainable long-term strategy.

Likewise, to believe that the impending departure of the UK from the EU will make this problem go away would be the very worst mistake that the remaining twenty-seven member states could make (Figure 14). At a time of populist party successes across the

14. **Europeans in the global community: national and EU heads at the G8, May 2012.**

continent and a more general revival of nationally framed (and nationalistic) politics, the need to accentuate the gains from working together is arguably greater than it has ever been in the EU's history. As the UK is going to discover in the coming years and decades, national economies and societies are deeply entwined with those of other countries, and the scope for unilateral action is very limited indeed: the EU offers a way for its members to face that challenge with a wider range of policy tools and a greater weight within the international system.

Flexible versus federal

All of which brings us back to the conceptualizations of integration that started us off in this short guide—to federalism and intergovernmentalism—albeit in a slightly different guise.

One of the more striking successes of the UK's involvement in the EU has been to promote the notion of 'flexibility': we might note the irony of the sixtieth anniversary declaration in Rome making much of this, even as its greatest proponent was absent, packing its bags (or, at least, writing the note to explain why things weren't working out). The word 'flexible' was used approvingly in much British discourse to denote both the avoidance of excessive regulation in the economy and, politically, an aversion to proposals, apart from completion of the single market, for common instruments and legally binding commitments.

Flexibility in the economic sense has been successful in the development of the swiftly changing contemporary economy; and this has been increasingly recognized in the EU. But flexibility in the political sense has had to balance the value of general applicability with the difficulty of reaching agreement in the first place. The recent challenges to some of the fundamental principles of the EU, including free movement and non-discrimination on the basis of nationality, have demonstrated the need for collective action, the better to protect the rights of all members.

The Eurozone crisis has shown very vividly the extent to which national economies are deeply interlinked and interdependent. Thus the ability of the Eurozone to find lasting solutions to its problems is of interest not only to its members, but also to all other EU member states, and beyond. One of the more difficult messages that has needed to be communicated is precisely that it is neither possible nor desirable to stand on the side-lines of events and urge others to do something. This is undoubtedly true in economic matters, although it does present many complications in both political and legal terms. As the crisis has shown all too well, even if a state is not formally within the system, then it is still affected by what happens and has a role to play in finding solutions: the UK will have ample opportunity to discover that leaving the EU does not mean that the EU is no longer important to its society and economy. When the UK does finally leave—probably in 2019—it will still find itself neighbouring an EU that buys British goods and services, but in which the British government no longer has an institutional voice (and vote).

The crises facing the EU present both a threat and an opportunity. Even if the British case is one that is currently unlikely to be directly replicated elsewhere, the lack of popular engagement is widespread. Moreover, the persistent failure of the EU to provide determined and effective action on points of policy in migration, employment, or public security all undermine the traditional output-based model of legitimacy: the idea that the EU was worth supporting because it did useful things. Likewise the absence of strong leadership on how to respond—from the Commission, European Council, or member states—is not simply a matter of the personalities involved, but also of the complexity of the task.

At the same time, it is possible to characterize much of the EU's history as one of crisis. In the points of rupture, disagreement, and stasis are buried the seeds of the next steps. If there is one historical lesson to be drawn, then it is that despite all the problems and difficulties on the way, states have persisted with this venture. With the exception of the UK, it is very hard to think of any occasions where members have sought to unwind what happens, instead they have worked together to find new alternatives for action, which has had the cumulative effect of building the European level of governance.

It is something of a truism to say that we live in an ever more interconnected world, but this does not make it any less true. From the economy to the environment, social problems to security—problems cross borders more and more. Therefore we should not be surprised that states look increasingly to pursuing solutions to those problems in a cross-border way too.

The challenge has been one of finding a democratic, effective, and sustainable way of doing this. A major difficulty has been the reluctance of many to accept the allocation of resources to the EU and to strengthen its institutions in ways that could make it sufficiently effective; something that implies the acceptance of an adequate core of legally binding commitments and common instruments, with institutional reform to make the EU properly effective and democratic. The word 'federal' is a convenient and accurate abbreviation for the words following 'core of' in the preceding sentence, whether or not such commitments, instruments, and reformed institutions lead eventually to a federation. The word is less important than what it represents. Its use, if properly defined, would, however, clarify thinking as well as facilitate communication with those who use it. A rose by any other name would smell as sweet. But it is better to give the rose a name consisting of one word rather than seventeen.

As the EU heads into its seventh decade of existence, the pains it is undergoing are more redolent of adolescence. The EU has much to offer in contributing to a safer and more prosperous world, but it will only be able to do that if it can find a way of bringing its citizens into a new model of participation and legitimacy. Whether

147

it can achieve that is as much in the balance as it has ever been. Perhaps in the loss of the UK will be born a greater awareness among European publics of what might be lost should the EU fall apart, but if it is to have a long-term future then a more positive formulation will have to be found. The path to maturity for the EU remains unclear and uncertain.

References

References, in line with the nature of this series, have been kept to the minimum of quotations whose source is not obvious from the text.

Chapter 2: How the EU was made

Spinelli called the Single Act a 'dead mouse' in his speech to the European Parliament on 16 January 1986, reprinted in Altiero Spinelli, *Discorsi al Parlamento Europeo*, ed. Pier Virgilio Dastoli (Bologna, 1987), p. 369. Jenkins recalled his choice of a theme to 'move Europe forward' in *European Diary 1977–1981* (London, 1989), pp. 22–3.

Chapter 3: How the EU is governed

Margaret Thatcher spoke of 'a European super-state' in her *Britain and Europe: Text of the Speech Delivered in Bruges by the Prime Minister on 20th September 1988* (London: Conservative Political Centre, 1988), p. 4.

Chapter 7: 'An area of freedom, security and justice'

Bevin and Victoria Station is to be found in Michael Charlton, *The Price of Victory* (London, 1983), pp. 43–4.

Chapter 9: The EU and the rest of Europe

Poos on 'the hour of Europe' was reported in the *New York Times*, 29 June 1991, p. 4.

Chapter 10: The EU in the world

The Community 'as an example' is from Jean Monnet, *Les États-Unis d'Europe ont commencé. Discours et allocutions 1952–1954* (Paris, 1955), p. 128.

The EC as 'the most important member of Gatt' is from Lawrence B. Krause, *European Economic Integration and the United States* (Washington, DC, 1968), p. 225.

The EC and 'effective international law-making' is from Tommaso Padoa-Schioppa, *Financial and Monetary Integration in Europe: 1990, 1992 and Beyond* (London and New York, 1990), p. 28.

Further reading

There is a great deal of academic literature on the EU, but not so many reliable books for the general reader or for those who are just setting out to acquire academic knowledge.

Of the many texts that provide general introductions, two good options are Michelle Cini and Nieves Pérez-Solórzano Borragán's *European Union Politics* (Oxford, 5th edn, 2016, 512 pp.) and John McCormick's *Understanding the EU* (Basingstoke, 7th edn, 2017, 252 pp.). A federalist view of the way in which the EU has developed is to be found in Michael Burgess, *Federalism and European Union: The Building of Europe, 1950–2000* (London, 2000, 290 pp.). Chapters on all the main policies are to be found in Helen Wallace, Mark Pollack, and Alisdair Young (eds), *Policy-Making in the European Union* (Oxford, 7th edn, 2014, 616 pp.). A wide range of subjects is also covered in the *Annual Review* of the *Journal of Common Market Studies* (Oxford).

For those who appreciate a biographical approach to the subject, the history of the EC up to the 1970s is seen through the eyes of its principal founding father in Jean Monnet's *Memoirs* (London, 1978, 544 pp.). Flavour and substance of the Delors period, from 1985 to 1994, are to be found in Charles Grant, *Inside the House that Jacques Built* (London, 1994, 305 pp.). A range of leading actors in the uniting of Europe are given lively treatment in Martyn Bond, Julie Smith, and William Wallace (eds), *Eminent Europeans* (London, 1996, 321 pp.). Hugo Young provides unsurpassed insights into the development of British relations with the EU, through chapters on a dozen British protagonists and antagonists from Churchill to Blair, in *This Blessed Plot* (Basingstoke, 1998, 558 pp.).

There is not much that is easy to read, and gives a true and fair view of how the institutions work. Simon Hix's *The Political System of the European Union* (Basingstoke, 3rd edn, 2011, 448 pp.) is insightful and well-argued, if now a bit dated. Dermot Hodson and John Peterson's *The Institutions of the European Union* (Oxford, 4th edn, 2017, 496 pp.) provides a very good overview.

For discussion of the nature and possibility of democracy in the EU, the most useful starting points are Simon Hix's *The Political System of the European Union* (Basingstoke, 3rd edn, 2011, 448 pp.) and Mette Eilstrup-Sangiovanni's *Debates on European Integration* (London, 2006, 512pp.), both of which cover the breadth of the debate.

Richard Baldwin and Charles Wyplosz's *The Economics of European Integration* (London, 5th edn, 560 pp.) has the most current overview of economics and economic policies. Lord Cockfield's *The European Union: Creating the Single Market* (Chichester, 1994, 185 pp.) is a lucid and entertaining account by the man who did most to create it. The budget is well-explained by Brigid Laffan and Johannes Lindner's 'The Budget' (in Helen Wallace, Mark Pollack, and Alisdair Young (eds), *Policy-Making in the European Union* (Oxford, 7th edn, 2014, 616 pp.).

Most of the literature on the EU's external relations is about the Common Foreign and Security Policy, though the external economic policies remain more effective and important. A good starting point is Amelia Hadfield, Ian Manners, and Richard Whitman's *Foreign Policies of the EU Member States* (Basingstoke, 2017, 296 pp.).

The Area of Freedom, Security and Justice is also a fast-moving subject: Sandra Lavenex's chapter on 'Justice and Home Affairs' (in Helen Wallace, Mark Pollack, and Alisdair Young (eds), *Policy-Making in the European Union* (Oxford, 7th edn, 2014, 616 pp.) gives a good overview.

Across the board, the EU's website <http://europa.eu> is a vast quarry of information, from the very basic through to the highly technical.

Chronology: 1946–2017

1940s

19 September 1946	Churchill calls for 'a kind of United States of Europe'.
16 April 1948	OEEC (later OECD) created to coordinate Marshall Plan for Western European states.
4 April 1949	Signature of North Atlantic Treaty establishing Nato.
5 May 1949	Establishment of Council of Europe.

1950s

9 May 1950	Schuman Declaration launches negotiations to establish ECSC, as 'a first step in the federation of Europe'.
18 April 1951	The Six (Belgium, France, Germany, Italy, Luxembourg, and Netherlands) sign ECSC Treaty.
27 May 1952	The Six sign EDC Treaty.
27 July 1952	ECSC Treaty enters into force.
30 August 1954	French National Assembly shelves EDC Treaty.
1–2 June 1955	Foreign ministers of the Six agree at Messina to launch negotiations resulting in EEC and Euratom.
25 March 1957	Rome Treaties establishing EEC and Euratom signed.
1 January 1958	Rome Treaties enter into force.

1960s

3 May 1960	Efta established by Austria, Denmark, Norway, Portugal, Sweden, Switzerland, and UK.
31 July, 10 August 1961	Ireland, Denmark, and UK apply to join EC. Norway applies in April 1962.
14 January 1963	President de Gaulle terminates accession negotiations.
1 July 1965	France breaks off negotiations on financing CAP and boycotts European Council until January 1966.
28–9 January 1966	Luxembourg 'Compromise' agreed. France returns to European Council insisting on unanimity when 'very important' interests at stake.
11 May 1967	UK reactivates membership application followed by Ireland, Denmark, and Norway. De Gaulle still demurs.

1970s

22 April 1970	Amending Treaty signed, giving EC all revenue from common external tariff and agricultural import levies plus share of VAT, and European Parliament some powers over budget.
27 October 1970	European Council establishes EPC procedures for foreign policy cooperation.
1 January 1973	Denmark, Ireland, and UK join EC.
9–10 December 1974	Paris Summit decides to hold meetings three times a year as European Council and gives go-ahead for direct elections to European Parliament.
28 February 1975	EC and forty-six African, Caribbean, and Pacific countries sign Lomé Convention.
18 March 1975	ERDF established.
22 July 1975	Amending Treaty signed, giving European Parliament more budgetary powers and setting up Court of Auditors.

| 4-5 December 1978 | European Council establishes EMS with ERM based on ecu. |
| 7, 10 June 1979 | First direct elections to European Parliament. |

1980s

1 January 1981	Greece becomes tenth member of EC.
14 February 1984	Draft Treaty on EU, inspired by Spinelli, passed by large majority in European Parliament.
25-6 June 1984	Fontainebleau European Council agrees on rebate to reduce UK's net contribution to EC budget.
14 June 1985	Schengen Agreement eliminating border controls signed by Belgium, France, Germany, Luxembourg, Netherlands.
28-9 June 1985	European Council approves Commission project to complete single market by 1992; considers proposals from Parliament's Draft Treaty; initiates IGC for treaty amendment.
1 January 1986	Spain, Portugal accede, membership now twelve.
17, 28 February 1986	SEA signed.
1 July 1987	SEA enters into force.
9 November 1989	Fall of Berlin Wall. German Democratic Republic opens borders.
8-9 December 1989	European Council initiates IGC on Emu; all save UK adopt charter of workers' social rights.

1990s

| 3 October 1990 | Unification of Germany and de facto enlargement of EC. |
| 14-15 December 1990 | European Council launches IGCs on Emu and political union. |

9–10 December 1991	European Council agrees TEU (Maastricht Treaty).
16 December 1991	'Europe Agreements' with Poland, Hungary, and Czechoslovakia signed; those with Czech Republic and Slovakia (successors to Czechoslovakia), Bulgaria, Estonia, Latvia, Lithuania, Romania, and Slovenia follow at intervals.
7 February 1992	Maastricht Treaty signed.
2 May 1992	Agreement on EEA signed.
2 June 1992	Danish referendum rejects Maastricht Treaty.
11–12 December 1992	European Council offers Denmark special arrangements to facilitate treaty ratification; endorses Delors package of budgetary proposals; agrees to start accession negotiations with Austria, Norway, Sweden, and Finland.
31 December 1992	Bulk of single market legislation completed on time.
18 May 1993	Second Danish referendum accepts Maastricht Treaty.
21–2 June 1993	Copenhagen European Council declares associated Central and Eastern European states can join when they fulfil the political and economic conditions.
1 November 1993	Maastricht Treaty enters into force.
1 January 1995	Austria, Finland, and Sweden join, membership now fifteen.
26 July 1995	Member states sign Europol Convention.
2 October 1997	Amsterdam Treaty signed.
1 June 1998	ECB established.
1 January 1999	Euro becomes official currency of Austria, Belgium, Finland, France, Germany, Ireland, Italy, Luxembourg, Netherlands, Portugal, and Spain.
15 March 1999	Commission resigns following report by independent committee on allegations of mismanagement and fraud.
1 May 1999	Amsterdam Treaty enters into force.

10–11 December 1999	European Council initiates IGC for treaty revision.

2000s

15 January 2000	Accession negotiations open with Bulgaria, Latvia, Lithuania, Malta, Romania, and Slovakia.
20 June 2000	Lisbon European Council agrees measures for flexibility in EU economy.
7–10 December 2000	European Council concludes negotiations for Nice Treaty and proclaims Charter of Fundamental Rights.
1 January 2001	Greece becomes twelfth member of euro zone.
14–15 December 2001	Laeken European Council agrees declaration on future of EU, opening way for a wholesale reform process.
1 January 2002	Euro notes and coins enter into circulation.
28 February 2002	Convention on Future of EU opens in Brussels.
12–13 December 2002	Copenhagen European Council concludes accession negotiations with ten countries in Central and Eastern Europe and the Mediterranean.
1 February 2003	Treaty of Nice enters into force.
4 October 2003	IGC opens to consider treaty reform on basis of Convention's draft EU constitution.
1 May 2004	Cyprus, Czech Republic, Estonia, Hungary, Latvia, Lithuania, Malta, Poland, Slovakia, and Slovenia join EU, making twenty-five member states.
29 October 2004	Heads of state and government and EU foreign ministers sign treaty establishing Constitution for Europe.
29 May, 1 June 2005	French and Dutch voters reject Constitutional Treaty in referendums.
3 October 2005	Accession negotiations open with Turkey and Croatia.

1 January 2007	Bulgaria and Romania become twenty-sixth and twenty-seventh member states of EU. Slovenia becomes thirteenth participant in Eurozone.
23 July 2007	Opening of IGC on Lisbon Treaty.
13 December 2007	Signing of Lisbon Treaty
21 December 2007	Enlargement of Schengen area to Estonia, Czech Republic, Lithuania, Hungary, Latvia, Malta, Poland, Slovakia, and Slovenia.
1 January 2008	Cyprus and Malta adopt euro.
12 December 2008	Switzerland joins Schengen area.
1 January 2009	Slovakia joins euro.
20 November 2009	Appointment of Herman van Rompuy as first President of European Council and of Catherine Ashton as High Representative of EU for Foreign Affairs and Security Policy.
1 December 2009	Lisbon Treaty enters into force.

2010s

17 June 2010	Adoption of 'Europe 2020' strategy for sustainable growth over next ten years.
1 January 2011	Estonia adopts euro. Start of operations for new financial supervisory bodies: European Banking Authority, European Insurance and Occupational Pensions Authority, and European Securities and Markets Authority.
18 January 2011	Start of first 'European semester' of economic policy coordination by member states.
25 March 2011	Euro Plus Pact agreed.
11 July 2011	Eurozone members sign Treaty on ESM, to act as a reserve for states in financial crisis.
21 July 2011	First round of support for Greek economy of €109 billion.

8 November 2011	Adoption of 'six-pack' of legislation on economic governance.
30 January 2012	New Treaty on Stability, Coordination and Governance is agreed by all member states except Czech Republic and UK.
21 February 2012	Second round of support for Greek economy.
1 March 2012	Serbia given candidate status.
1 April 2012	European Citizens' Initiative comes into force, enabling citizens to propose EU legislation.
1 July 2013	Croatia becomes twenty-eighth member state.
1 January 2014	Latvia joins euro.
4 November 2014	Single Supervisory Mechanism enters into force.
1 January 2015	Lithuania joins euro.
19 August 2015	Third round of support for Greek economy.
1 January 2016	Single Resolution Mechanism enters into force.
23 June 2016	UK referendum on EU membership results in decision to leave.
29 March 2017	UK submits notification to begin process of leaving EU.

Glossary

Words in *italics* refer to other entries.

accession: The process of joining the *EU*. After accession treaties have been negotiated, all member states must ratify them and the *EP* must give its assent.

Acquis Communautaire: The full set of the *EU*'s legislative, regulatory, judicial, and normative output.

AFSJ (Area of Freedom, Security and Justice): Policies relating to coordination of internal security and justice systems.

asymmetric shocks: Affect different regions within an economy in different ways—a potential problem for the *Eurozone*.

Brexit ('British exit'): The UK's withdrawal from the *EU*.

budget of the EU: Revenue comes from *own resources*; two-thirds of spending is on the *CAP* and *cohesion policy*.

CAP (common agricultural policy): Much reformed, it still accounts for 40 per cent of the *EU*'s budget spending, through its direct support of farmers and rural development.

CFSP (Common Foreign and Security Policy): Originally, the second pillar of the *EU*, for intergovernmental cooperation on foreign policy. Now an integral part of the *EU*.

citizenship: The *TEU* created a European citizenship, alongside member states' citizenships. Citizens are entitled to rights conferred by the treaties.

CJHA (Cooperation in Justice and Home Affairs): Former third pillar of the *EU*, for cooperation relating to movement of people across frontiers and for combating cross-frontier crime.

cohesion policy: The *EU*'s regional development policy, implemented through *structural funds* accounting for one-third of *EU budget* spending.

comitology: System of committees of member states' officials supervising the *Commission*'s work on behalf of the *Council of Ministers*. Now largely replaced by *implementing acts*.

Commission (European Commission): The main executive body of the *EU*, comprising twenty-eight commissioners, responsible for different policy areas. In addition to its executive functions, the Commission initiates legislation and supervises compliance. The term 'Commission' is often used collectively for the Commission and its staff.

Committee of the Regions: Comprises representatives of regional and local authorities. Provides opinions on legislation and issues reports on its own initiative.

Community: See *EC* and *EEC*.

Constitutional Treaty: A proposed treaty revision, based on the work of the *Convention on the Future of Europe*, but rejected following referendums in 2005 in France and the Netherlands, despite ratification by the majority of member states. Most of its provisions were eventually incorporated into the *Lisbon Treaty*.

Convention on the Future of Europe: Open forum of representatives of parliaments and governments set up in 2002 after the Laeken declaration by the *European Council* to discuss a complete redrawing of the *EU*. Under its chair, Valéry Giscard d'Estaing, it presented a Draft Treaty establishing a Constitution for Europe in 2003, which formed the basis of the *Constitutional Treaty*.

Copenhagen Criteria: The benchmarks used by the *EU* for evaluating the suitability of states applying for membership. They cover: stable institutions guaranteeing democracy, the rule of law, human rights and respect for minorities; a functioning market economy; the ability to take on the *acquis*, and support for the various aims of the *EU*.

Coreper (Committee of Permanent Representatives): See *Council of Ministers*.

Council of Ministers: Comprises representatives of member states at ministerial level. It amends and *votes* on legislation, supervises execution of policies. It is supported by the Council Secretariat in Brussels, and by *Coreper* and its system of committees (see *comitology*). The *Council of Ministers*, with the *European Council*, is the *EU*'s most powerful political institution.

Court of Justice: The final judicial authority with respect to *EU* law. Its twenty-eight judges, one from each member state, sitting in Luxembourg, have developed an extensive case-law (see *direct effect* and *primacy*). The Court has ensured that the rule of law prevails in the *EU*.

CSDP (Common Security and Defence Policy): The defence and military cooperation element of *CFSP*.

direct effect: A core principle of the Court of Justice's jurisprudence that means individuals are able to rely on their rights under EC law in the same way as member states' laws.

directive: An *EU* legal act that is 'binding, as to the result to be achieved', but leaves to member states' authorities 'the choice of form and methods'.

EC (European Community): The central pillar of the *EU*, as laid out in the *Maastricht Treaty*. Incorporating the *EEC*, the *ECSC*, and *Euratom*, it contained federal elements of the *EU* institutions and was responsible for the bulk of *EU* activities. With the *Lisbon Treaty*, the EC is now fully integrated with the rest of the *EU*.

ECB (European Central Bank): Responsible for monetary policy for the *Eurozone*. Based in Frankfurt, the ECB is run by an Executive Board. Its members and the governors of central banks in the *Eurozone* comprise ECB's Governing Council. ECB and central banks together form the ESCB (European System of Central Banks), whose primary objective is to maintain price stability. None of these participants may take instructions from any other body.

ECJ (European Court of Justice): See *Court of Justice*.

Ecosoc (Economic and Social Committee): Comprises representatives of employers, workers, and social groups. Provides opinions on *EU* legislation and issues reports on its own initiative.

ECSC (European Coal and Steel Community): Launched by the Schuman Declaration of 9 May 1950, placing coal and steel sectors of six states (Belgium, France, Germany, Italy, Luxembourg, Netherlands) under a system of common governance. The *EEC* and *Euratom* were based on the ECSC's institutional structure. The treaty lapsed in 2002.

EDC (European Defence Community): A bold attempt in the early 1950s to integrate the armed forces of the *ECSC* states, shelved by the French National Assembly.

EEC (European Economic Community): Established in 1958 by the *Treaty of Rome*, its competences included the creation of a common market among the six member states and wide-ranging economic policy cooperation. Its main institutions were the *Commission*, *Council of Ministers*, *EP*, *Court of Justice*. It is the basis for today's *EU*.

Emu (Economic and Monetary Union): Seventeen member states participate in Emu, having satisfied the 'convergence criteria' of sound finance and irrevocably fixed their exchange rates with the euro, which replaced their currencies at the beginning of 2002. Monetary policy is the responsibility of the *European Central Bank* and the *ESCB*. There is a system for coordination of economic policy.

enhanced cooperation: Allows those states that want to integrate more closely than others in particular fields to do so within the *EU* framework.

EP (European Parliament): The directly elected body of the *EU*, its *MEPs* have substantial powers over *legislation*, the *budget*, and the *Commission*.

ESCB (European System of Central Banks): See *ECB*.

ESM (European Stability Mechanism): The permanent body set up in 2012 to provide emergency financial support to *Eurozone* member states in economic difficulty.

EU (European Union): Created by the *TEU*, with two new pillars alongside the central *EC* pillar, for cooperation in foreign and security policy and in 'justice and home affairs'. While the three pillars shared common institutions, the two new ones were predominantly intergovernmental. Since the *Lisbon Treaty*, the pillars are collapsed into one, with some residual differences in procedures between policy areas.

Euratom (European Atomic Energy Community): Established in 1957 alongside the *EEC* to promote cooperation in the field of atomic energy; undertakes research and development for civilian purposes.

European Commission: See *Commission*.

European Convention on Human Rights and Fundamental Freedoms: A framework for the protection of human rights across Europe, adopted in 1950 by the *Council of Europe*. *EU* states are all signatories and it is a basis for the respect of human rights in the *EU*. The *EU*'s Charter of Fundamental Rights is based in large part on the Convention.

European Council: Comprises the president of the European Council, heads of state and government of the member states, and president of the *Commission*. Takes decisions that require resolution or impetus at that level and defines political guidelines for the *EU*.

Eurozone: The area covered by the euro, the *EU*'s single currency.

federation: A federal polity is one in which the functions of government are divided between democratic institutions at two or more levels. The powers are usually divided according to the principle of *subsidiarity*, the member states or constituent parts having those powers that they can manage effectively.

Fiscal Compact: The 2012 treaty signed outside the *EU*'s legal order between most member states to enshrine balanced national budgets, with oversight by the *Commission*. Formally called the Treaty on Stability, Coordination and Governance in the *Emu* (TSCG).

free movement: The treaties provide for free movement within the *EU* of people, goods, capital, and services, known as 'the four freedoms', which together form the basis of the single market.

General Court: Judges cases brought by individuals, as well as those relating to competition policy, trade mark law, and state aids. Decisions can be appealed to the *Court of Justice*.

IGC (Intergovernmental Conference): The main way in which the *EU*'s treaties are revised. Member states' representatives in the IGC draft an amending treaty, which must be ratified by each state before it enters into force.

implementing acts: The system for oversight of implementation of *EU* legislation by member states, as introduced by the Lisbon Treaty.

legislative procedures: Most *EU* laws are enacted under the Ordinary Legislative Procedure, giving both the *EP* and *Council of Ministers* powers to accept, amend, or reject legislation. The cooperation procedure, which gave the *EP* less power, is no longer important; but the consultation procedure, where the *EP* is merely informed of *Council of Ministers*' intentions, is still quite widely applicable. The consent (formerly assent) procedure gives the *EP* powers over *accession* treaties, association agreements, and some legislative matters.

Maastricht Treaty: See *TEU*.

MEPs (Members of the European Parliament): Currently 754 MEPs are elected to the *EP* from across the member states. MEPs represent their constituents; scrutinize legislation in committees; vote on laws and the budget; supervise the *Commission*; debate the range of *EU* affairs.

Nato (North Atlantic Treaty Organization): Founded in 1949 as the security umbrella for Western Europe, tying in the US to the European security system.

open method of coordination: An increasingly common means of getting member states to share information and best practices without the use of legislation.

own resources: The tax revenue for the *budget of the EU*. The main sources are percentages of member states' GNPs and of the base for VAT; smaller amounts come from external tariffs and agricultural import levies.

permanent representations: Each member state has a permanent representation in Brussels, which is a centre for its interaction with the *EU*. The head of the representation is the state's representative in *Coreper* (see *Council of Ministers*).

Petersberg tasks: The military and security priorities for the *EU*'s foreign policy. They include humanitarian and rescue tasks, peacekeeping, and crisis management.

Police and Judicial Cooperation in Criminal Matters: See *CJHA*.

presidency: The *Council of Ministers* is chaired by representatives of one of the member states, on a six-month rotating basis.

primacy: A key principle of the *Court of Justice*, whereby *EU* law comes before national law, to ensure a uniform application of the former.

QMV (qualified majority voting): See *voting*.

regulation: An *EC* legal act that is 'binding in its entirety and directly applicable' in all member states.

Schengen Agreements: Originating in 1985 outside the *EU*, the Schengen Agreements now cover all member states save Ireland, the

UK, and to some extent Denmark. The Agreements have been incorporated in the *EU*.

SEA (Single European Act): Signed in 1986, the first major reform of the Rome Treaty. It provided for the 1992 programme to complete the single market; added some new competences; extended the use of *QMV*; enhanced the role of the *EP*.

secondary legislation: Laws enacted by the institutions within the powers given them by the treaties.

structural funds: Cohesion Fund, Regional Development Fund, Social Fund (see *cohesion policy*).

subsidiarity: A principle requiring action to be taken at *EU* level only when it can be more effective than action by individual states.

TEU (Treaty on European Union): Signed in 1991 at Maastricht, it established the *EU*. It laid down the procedures for creating *Emu*; gave *EP* important new powers; introduced a European *citizenship*; set up two new pillars, for *CFSP* and *CJHA*.

Treaties of Rome: See *EEC* and *Euratom*. The EEC Treaty is often called 'the Treaty of Rome'.

Treaty of Amsterdam: Signed in 1997, it extended the scope of co-decision and reformed the pillars on foreign policy and on justice and home affairs.

Treaty of Lisbon: Signed in 2007, it collapses the *EU*'s pillars, creates a new legal personality for the *EU*, revises decision-making procedures, and creates new offices for a president of the *European Council* and a high representative for foreign affairs and security policy. It draws significantly on the work of the *Convention on the Future of Europe* and the failed *Constitutional Treaty*.

Treaty of Nice: Signed in 2001, the Nice Treaty provided for institutional reforms in anticipation of the enlargement to Central and Eastern Europe, with new *voting* weights and procedures, and more use for *enhanced cooperation* procedures.

Union: See EU.

voting: Most decisions in the *Council of Ministers* are taken by *QMV*, which requires super-majorities of member states and of population. Unanimity applies less frequently to *EU* legislation but is more common in politically sensitive fields. Voting by simple majority is rare and mainly limited to procedural matters.

Glossary

WEU (Western European Union): Created in 1954 by the UK and *EC* member states. After a long period of inaction, the *Maastricht* and *Amsterdam* Treaties provided for links between the *EU* and WEU, which became incorporated into the *EU*. The WEU was declared defunct in 2011.

WTO (World Trade Organization): The 1995 successor to Gatt, WTO regulates international trade. It aims to reduce barriers to international trade and has mechanisms for resolving disputes.

Index

A

accession, conditions of 109–10
    see also enlargement
ACP (African, Caribbean, and
    Pacific) countries 125–7
Acquis Communautaire 60
Agenda 2000 28
Albania 116
Amsterdam Treaty 26–7
Area of Freedom, Security and
    Justice (AFSJ) 89–95
    see also border controls,
        Co-operation in Justice and
        Home Affairs, Police and
        Judicial Co-operation in
        Criminal Matters
Armenia 116
ASEAN 131
assent procedure 21, 100, 110
association agreements 27, 100,
    110, 116, 119, 125
asylum policy 90–4
Austria 26, 80, 107, 110–11

B

Belarus 116
Belgium 3, 4, 12, 90, 125
Bevin, Ernest 89

Blair, Tony 27
Bolkestein directive 61
border controls 89–94
    see also Area of Freedom,
        Security and Justice, Schengen
        Agreements
Bosnia-Herzegovina 115, 133–4
Brandt, Willy 16, 23
Brexit 55, 92, 115, 143–8
Britain 5, 14, 16–18, 20, 25, 27,
    43, 49, 55, 61, 69, 74, 84–5,
    90–2, 97, 106, 115, 122, 129,
    143–8
    entry into EC 5, 16–18
    Exchange Rate Mechanism 61–4
    opposition to single currency 25
    rebate of net contribution 69–71
    security 97, 106
    withdrawal from EU 55, 92, 115,
        143–8
budget 15–17, 43–6, 77–82
    European Parliament's
        powers 43–5
    generalized system of
        corrections 80
    net contributions 79–82
    rebate of British net
        contribution 69–71
    tax revenue 78–9
Bulgaria 28, 113

C

carbon and energy tax 88

'Cassis de Dijon' case 51, 60

Central and Eastern Europe, *see* enlargement, Eastern

Charter of Fundamental Rights 28, 30, 54, 92, 94, 143

Churchill, Winston 5, 6

citizenship 53–5

climate change 87–8, 101, 134

Cockfield, Lord 20, 59

co-decision procedure 23, 26, 28, 43, 86, 142

Cohesion Fund 75

cohesion policy 21, 72–7
see also structural funds

Committee of Permanent Representatives (Coreper) 38

common agricultural policy (CAP) 9–10, 14, 28, 69–73, 98, 122–3
reform 70–3

common commercial policy, *see* trade policy

common external tariff 5, 14, 57, 98, 121, 139–40

Common Foreign and Security Policy (CFSP) 25, 96–108
see also defence, European Political Co-operation, European Security and Defence Policy, security

common market 4–5, 12, 56
see also single market

Commonwealth countries 14, 125, 129

Commonwealth of Independent States (CIS) 116–17

competition policy 57–8

constitution 10, 20, 31

Constitutional Treaty 29–30, 61

Convention on the Future of Europe 28–30, 54

convergence criteria 63–4

Co-operation in Justice and Home Affairs (CJHA) 25, 89–93
see also Area of Freedom, Security and Justice

Copenhagen criteria 112

Cotonou agreement 125–9

Council of Ministers 34–40
effectiveness of 38, 141–2
executive powers 40
meetings of 38–9
qualified majority voting (QMV) 38–9

Court of First Instance 51

Court of Justice 50–1
rule of law 16

Croatia 115–16

customs union 13, 56–8

Cyprus 26, 113

Czech Republic 27, 30, 113

D

deepening 16, 28, 101

defence 96–108
European Defence Community 4
rapid reaction force 106–7
see also European Security and Defence Policy, security

de Gaulle, Charles 14–16

Delors, Jacques 10, 19, 23, 46, 59, 75, 111

democracy 3, 8, 10, 17, 54, 108, 112, 141–8

Denmark 14, 16–18, 25, 27, 53, 62, 92

deregulation 65, 85

development aid 100, 131–2
European Development Fund (EDF) 125

Directive 52

discrimination 54, 145

Doha round 123–4

Draft Treaty on European Union 20

E

Economic and Financial Council (Ecofin) 37
economic integration, *see* economic and monetary union, single currency, single market
economic and monetary union (Emu) 61–8
  external monetary policy 101
  institutions of 62–3
  see also euro, single currency
employment policies 26, 83–6
enhanced co-operation 27, 53
enlargement 3, 24, 109–15
  Britain, Denmark, Ireland 16–18
  conditions of accession 109–11
  Eastern 27–8, 111–15
  fatigue 109
  Northern enlargement 26
  Southern enlargement 21
  veto against 15
environmental policy 86–8, 139–40
equal pay 12, 54, 84
Estonia 65, 113
euro 61–2
  see also economic and monetary union, opt-outs, single currency
Euro-American relations, *see* United States
Euro-Mediterranean Policy (EMP) 129
European Agricultural Guarantee and Guidance Fund (EAGGF) 74
European Atomic Energy Community (Euratom) 12–14
European Central Bank (ECB) 62–3
European Coal and Steel Community (ECSC) 1, 4, 7, 10, 13
European Commission 13, 35, 45–50
  President of 45–7
  reform 46–8
European Community (EC) 2
  see also European Economic Community, European Union
European Convention on Human Rights 54
European Council 11, 17, 34–7
European Currency Unit (Ecu) 63
European Defence Community 4, 12
European Development Fund (EDF) 125
European Economic Area (EEA) 25, 111
European Economic Community (EEC) 2–5, 13
European Financial Stability Facility 66
European Free Trade Association (Efta) 90, 110
European Monetary System (EMS) 19
European Neighbourhood Policy (ENP) 129
European Parliament 15, 40–5
  control over European Commission 49
  direct elections to 17, 40
  Draft Treaty on European Union 20
  Members of (MEPs) 41–3
  party groups 41–2
  powers of, *see* assent procedure, budget, co-decision procedure
European Political Co-operation (EPC) 101–3
European Regional Development Fund (ERDF) 74
European Security and Defence Policy (ESDP) 107–8
European Stability Mechanism 67–8
European System of Central Banks (ESCB) 62–3

Index

European Union (EU) 13, 23–5
  founding treaties 23–5
Europol 91, 93
exchange rate co-operation 19
  Exchange Rate Mechanism
    (ERM) 61

F

federalism 3, 7–8, 10–15, 19–25,
  29, 145–8
Finland 26, 107
flexibility 27, 53
  see also enhanced co-operation,
    opt-outs
foreign policy, see Common Foreign
  and Security Policy, European
  Political Co-operation
founding treaties 13
France 1–5, 12, 14–15, 23, 62, 96–7,
  101–2, 125
  assistance to colonies 125
  Franco-German partnership 12,
    23, 102, 103
free movement, see border
  controls
frontier controls, see border
  controls

G

Gatt (General Agreement on Tariffs
  and Trade) 121–6
General Affairs Council 37
General Court 51
Generalized System of Preferences
  (GSP) 129–31
Georgia 133
German Democratic Republic 111
Germany 1–5, 12, 16, 23, 48, 62,
  96, 102–3
  Franco-German partnership 12,
    23, 102, 103
  Unification 111–12

Giscard d'Estaing, Valéry 17, 29
global warming, see climate
  change
Greece 21, 31, 60, 64, 66, 110

H

Hallstein, Walter 14
Heath, Edward 17, 18, 74
High Representative 31, 36–7, 47,
  55, 104–7
human rights 53–4
  Charter of Fundamental
    Rights 28, 30, 54, 92,
    94, 143
  European Convention 54
Hungary 28, 113, 115

I

immigration 91–4, 115
inflation 63
institutions 34–55
  see also individual institutions
Intergovernmental
  Conferences (IGCs) 20–1,
    26, 28, 102
intergovernmentalism 6–7
Iraq 108, 115
Ireland 14, 17, 27, 30, 60, 74, 90,
  92, 107
Italy 3, 64, 73

J

Justice and Home Affairs,
    see Co-operation in Justice and
    Home Affairs

K

Kohl, Helmut 23, 102
Kosovo 106, 115
Kyoto protocol 87–8

L

Laeken declaration 28–9
Latin America 129–32
Latvia 28, 65, 113
Liechtenstein 111
Lisbon treaty 13, 30–1, 38, 40, 43–4, 47, 52, 55, 92, 104, 107, 142
Lithuania 28, 65, 113
Lomé Convention 125–6
Luxembourg 3
Luxembourg 'compromise' 15–16

M

Maastricht Treaty 23–6
Macedonia 116, 133
MacSharry, Ray 71
Major, John 25
Malta 26, 113
Members of the European Parliament (MEPs) 28, 40–1, 44
migration crisis 94, 115, 146
Mitterrand, François 20, 23, 102
Mogherini, Federica 104
Moldova 116
Monnet, Jean 10–11
Montenegro 116

N

Nato 103–7, 132–3
neo-functionalism 7–8
neo-realism 7
net contributions 79–82
Netherlands 3, 80, 125
Nice Treaty 28
non-tariff barriers 20, 58–60, 122
Norway 16–17, 26, 111

O

opt-outs 27, 53
    border controls 90
    single currency 53, 62
    social policy 85
own resources 78–9

P

peace, as motive for EU 1
Petersberg tasks 115
PHARE programme 112
Poland 28, 113
Police and Judicial Co-operation in Criminal Matters 25, 92–3
    see also Area of Freedom, Security and Justice
Portugal 21, 60, 74, 110, 131
Presidency of the Council of Ministers 31, 35
presidency conclusions 37
Putin, Vladimir 117

Q

qualified majority voting (QMV) 38–9, 48
quotas 57, 69

R

rapid reaction force 106–7
Regulation 52
Romania 28, 113
Rome Treaties, see Treaties of Rome
rule of law, see Court of Justice
Russia 116–17

S

Schengen Agreements 90, 140
Schuman declaration 2

Schuman, Robert 2
security, external 96–108
　see also Common Foreign
　　and Security Policy,
　　European Security and
　　Defence Policy
security, internal, *see* Area
　of Freedom, Security and
　Justice, Co-operation
　in Justice and Home
　Affairs, Police and Judicial
　Co-operation in Criminal
　Matters
Serbia 116
single currency 61–2
　see also economic and monetary
　　union, euro
Single European Act (SEA) 21, 38,
　54, 84, 89
Single Farm Payment 73
single market 56–61
Slovakia 28, 113
Slovenia 28, 113
social chapter 25, 85
Social Charter 84
Social Fund 12, 73
social policy 83–6
Solana, Javier 104
Soviet Union 16, 111
Spain 21, 60, 74, 76, 110
spillover 7
Spinelli, Altiero 10, 20, 22
Stability and Growth
　Pact 66
Stability Pact for South-East
　Europe 116
state aids 58
structural funds 73–7
　see also Social Fund
subsidiarity 52–3, 60
subsidies 58, 70, 98
Sweden 26
Switzerland 26, 111

tariffs 57
　see also common external tariff
Technical Assistance to the
　Commonwealth of Independent
　States (TACIS) 117
terrorism 32, 91, 93
Thatcher, Margaret 17, 19–20, 23, 52
trade policy 98–101
Treaties of Rome 13
Treaty on Stability, Coordination
　and Governance 67
Trevi agreement 90
Turkey 119–20

Ukraine 116–17
unanimity procedure 38
unemployment, *see* employment
　policies
United Kingdom, *see* Britain
United States 132–7

V

veto 38
　see also Luxembourg 'compromise'

West Balkans 106, 116
widening, *see* enlargement
Wilson, Harold 17
women, equal treatment of 54, 84
World Trade Organization
　(WTO) 72–3
World War II 1–3

Y

Yugoslavia 115

INTERNATIONAL RELATIONS

A Very Short Introduction
Paul Wilkinson

Of undoubtable relevance today, in a post-9-11 world of growing political tension and unease, this *Very Short Introduction* covers the topics essential to an understanding of modern international relations. Paul Wilkinson explains the theories and the practice that underlies the subject, and investigates issues ranging from foreign policy, arms control, and terrorism, to the environment and world poverty. He examines the role of organizations such as the United Nations and the European Union, as well as the influence of ethnic and religious movements and terrorist groups which also play a role in shaping the way states and governments interact. This up-to-date book is required reading for those seeking a new perspective to help untangle and decipher international events.

www.oup.com/vsi

THE FIRST WORLD WAR
A Very Short Introduction
Michael Howard

By the time the First World War ended in 1918, eight million people had died in what had been perhaps the most apocalyptic episode the world had known. This *Very Short Introduction* provides a concise and insightful history of the 'Great War', focusing on why it happened, how it was fought, and why it had the consequences it did. It examines the state of Europe in 1914 and the outbreak of war; the onset of attrition and crisis; the role of the US; the collapse of Russia; and the weakening and eventual surrender of the Central Powers. Looking at the historical controversies surrounding the causes and conduct of war, Michael Howard also describes how peace was ultimately made, and the potent legacy of resentment left to Germany.

'succinct, comprehensive and beautifully written. Indeed reading it is an experience comparable to scanning the clues of a well-composed crossword puzzle. Every allusion is eventually supplied with an answer, and the finished product defies the puzzler's disbelief that the intricacies can be brought to a convincing conclusion. . . . Michael Howard is the master of the short book'

TLS

www.oup.com/vsi

DIPLOMACY
A Very Short Introduction
Joseph M. Siracusa

Like making war, diplomacy has been around a very long time, at least since the Bronze Age. It was primitive by today's standards, there were few rules, but it was a recognizable form of diplomacy. Since then, diplomacy has evolved greatly, coming to mean different things, to different persons, at different times, ranging from the elegant to the inelegant. Whatever one's definition, few could doubt that the course and consequences of the major events of modern international diplomacy have shaped and changed the global world in which we live. Joseph M. Siracusa introduces the subject of diplomacy from a historical perspective, providing examples from significant historical phases and episodes to illustrate the art of diplomacy in action.

'Professor Siracusa provides a lively introduction to diplomacy through the perspective of history.'

Gerry Woodard, Senior Fellow in Political Science at the University of Melbourne and former Australasian Ambassador in Asia

www.oup.com/vsi

GLOBALIZATION
A Very Short Introduction
Manfred Steger

'Globalization' has become one of the defining buzzwords of our time - a term that describes a variety of accelerating economic, political, cultural, ideological, and environmental processes that are rapidly altering our experience of the world. It is by its nature a dynamic topic - and this *Very Short Introduction* has been fully updated for 2009, to include developments in global politics, the impact of terrorism, and environmental issues. Presenting globalization in accessible language as a multifaceted process encompassing global, regional, and local aspects of social life, Manfred B. Steger looks at its causes and effects, examines whether it is a new phenomenon, and explores the question of whether, ultimately, globalization is a good or a bad thing.

www.oup.com/vsi

Modern China
A Very Short Introduction
Rana Mitter

China today is never out of the news: from human rights controversies and the continued legacy of Tiananmen Square, to global coverage of the Beijing Olympics, and the Chinese 'economic miracle'. It seems a country of contradictions: a peasant society with some of the world's most futuristic cities, heir to an ancient civilization that is still trying to find a modern identity. This *Very Short Introduction* offers the reader with no previous knowledge of China a variety of ways to understand the world's most populous nation, giving a short, integrated picture of modern Chinese society, culture, economy, politics and art.

'A brilliant essay.'

Timothy Garton, TLS

MODERN JAPAN
A Very Short Introduction
Christopher Goto-Jones

Japan is arguably today's most successful industrial economy, combining almost unprecedented affluence with social stability and apparent harmony. Japanese goods and cultural products are consumed all over the world, ranging from animated movies and computer games all the way through to cars, semiconductors, and management techniques. In many ways, Japan is an icon of the modern world, and yet it remains something of an enigma to many, who see it as a confusing montage of the alien and the familiar, the ancient and modern. The aim of this Very Short Introduction is to explode the myths and explore the reality of modern Japan - by taking a concise look at its history, economy, politics, and culture.

> 'A wonderfully engaging narrative of a complicated history, which from the beginning to end sheds light on the meaning of modernity in Japan as it changed over time. An exemplary text.'
>
> Carol Gluck, Columbia University

www.oup.com/vsi